# THINKING
# ANTHROPOLOGICALLY

# THINKING ANTHROPOLOGICALLY

## A Practical Guide for Students

*PHILIP CARL SALZMAN*
MCGILL UNIVERSITY

*PATRICIA C. RICE*
WEST VIRGINIA UNIVERSITY

CO-EDITORS

Upper Saddle River, New Jersey 07458

*Library of Congress Cataloging-in-Publication Data*

Thinking anthropologically : a practical guide for students / Philip Carl Salzman and
   Patricia C. Rice, editors.
      p.   cm.
   ISBN 0-13-183520-3 (alk. paper)
      1. Anthropology–Philosophy.   2. Anthropology–Methodology. I. Salzman, Philip Carl.
   II. Rice, Patricia C.

GN33.T45   2003
301'.01–dc21

2003042855


*AVP/Publisher:* Nancy Roberts
*Production Editor:* Cheryl A. Keenan
*Copyeditor:* Carol Peschke
*Proofreader:* Beatrice Marcks
*Editorial Assistant:* Lee Peterson
*Prepress and Manufacturing Buyer:* Ben Smith
*Director of Marketing:* Beth Mejia
*Marketing Assistant:* Adam Laitman
*Cover Art Director:* Jayne Conte
*Cover Design:* Kiwi Design


This book was set in 10/12 Baskerville by Interactive Composition Corporation, Inc.,
and was printed and bound by Phoenix Book Tech.
The cover was printed by Phoenix Color Corp.

 © 2004 by Pearson Education Inc.
Upper Saddle River, New Jersey 07458

Printed in the United States of America
10 9 8 7 6 5 4 3 2


**ISBN: 0-13-183520-3**

Pearson Education LTD., London
Pearson Education Australia PTY, Limited, Sydney
Pearson Education Singapore, Pte. Ltd
Pearson Education North Asia Ltd, Hong Kong
Pearson Education Canada, Ltd., Toronto
Pearson Educación de Mexico, S.A. de C.V.
Pearson Education–Japan, Tokyo
Pearson Education Malaysia, Pte. Ltd
Pearson Education, Upper Saddle River, New Jersey

# Contents

# *THINKING ANTHROPOLOGICALLY*

# Introduction to Thinking Anthropologically

PHILIP CARL SALZMAN, *McGill University*

PATRICIA C. RICE, *West Virginia University*

## PART 1: FOR STUDENTS ONLY

When I (Salzman) was a freshman at Antioch College in Ohio, I took an introductory philosophy course. In preparing for each class, I usually read at least some of the assigned reading in the collection of selections from great philosophers. But when I got to class and the professor began talking about the assigned reading, I recognized nothing in what I had read from what he was saying. There seemed to be no overlap between what I understood from the text and what the professor was telling us it was about. I might as well have been reading *Dilbert*.

As you can imagine, this was a rather disconcerting experience. But in a way, it was inevitable. Why? Because I had no clue as to the frames of reference that philosophers used to situate their discussions. I did not know what philosophers thought were problems, how they intended to address them, or even what they thought would count as answers. In other words, I had no idea how to think philosophically.

When I (Rice) was an undergraduate up the road from Antioch College at Ohio State University, I took my first economics course and had an experience that was similar to that of my co-editor. What I read and what the instructor said, supposedly about the same material, were as different as night and day. The terminology was a kind of foreign language, but I could cope with that. What was

1

frustrating and unnerving was the fact that I hadn't a clue as to how to think economically. This did improve during the term, but not until an hour before the final
exam did it all become clear. At the time, I called it the "aha" syndrome, but I now
know that only at the last minute was I beginning to think economically. If I had
begun to think economically at the beginning of the course instead of at the end of
it, I am sure I would have been less frustrated and would have learned a good deal
more. We hope this book will help you to avoid that kind of experience by learning how to think anthropologically early in your first anthropological adventure in
the classroom.

Such frustrations occur in any new field that you study, whether physics, literature, history, or anthropology. When we begin to explore a new field, we enter
our exploration at one time and place, a little like taking the first steps off a beach
into a lake or sea. It is impossible for us to know all of the other points at which
we might have stepped into the water, the overall shape of the water body, and
how it affects the place into which we have stepped.

Your instructor, however knowledgeable and good at communicating, cannot
talk about everything at once. He or she cannot tell you at the same time about specific ethnographic cases and about different kinds of societies, or about epistemological assumptions about how we learn things at the same time as about ethnographic field work methods, or about general heuristic theories at the same time as
about specific understandings of particular cultural patterns. He or she cannot tell
you about Darwin and Mendel's contributions to evolution at the same time he or
she is discussing the details of *Australopithecus robustus,* much less the ecological context and why we think the population that this fossil represents adapted to life on
the savanna. You eventually need to know all of these things and how they influence
one another, but you cannot learn all of it at once. Be patient; you will catch on.

Well, we have a bit more to offer than "be patient." The short chapters in
this collection are clear explanations of the underlying frameworks assumed and
used by anthropologists. What does your instructor mean by "theory"? You will
find some answers to this in Chapter 4. When your instructor talks about studying culture, what does she or he mean? Chapter 2 will give you some clues to this
question. Why do anthropologists disagree, and how can you learn about
anthropology when anthropologists can't even agree among themselves? Chapter 7 discusses this issue. After you read these chapters, you will begin to **think
anthropologically.** This will help you understand your instructor and the assigned readings better and will help you do better in the course.

The authors of each chapter are teaching anthropologists who, like your instructor, see students who are brand new to anthropology every semester. Most
teach introductory courses as well as advanced courses in their specialities. They
all have their interests and biases and may not all agree that the theme of each
chapter is the single most important aspect of anthropology. For example, some
may be humanist anthropologists who believe descriptions of other cultures and
attempts to find cultural meaning are the most important part of anthropology,
whereas others are scientists who attempt to explain particular aspects of what it is

to be human. Some may feel ethics should be the focus of each topic, while others may limit ethics to professional audiences. Some feel very strongly that the importance and fun of anthropology lie in the interrelatedness of its parts—the past and the present, culture and biology—whereas others are perfectly happy teaching and researching only one subfield. Some feel very strongly that if we do not apply our knowledge, we are giving up an opportunity to help others, whereas some feel that our main obligation is increasing knowledge. And this profile fits anthropologists in general, not just the authors of these chapters. We all think anthropologically, however, and believe it is at the heart of what we do and what we teach. We want to share this experience with you while we impart some knowledge about what it is to be human.

We believe that this book will help you understand anthropology, but perhaps future editions can be even more useful. We would like to ask you to help us improve this book for future students by telling your instructor whether you found it helpful, which chapters were most useful, which ones were least useful, and what other subjects you wish had been covered. Working together, we can help other students to think anthropologically.

## PART 2: FOR INSTRUCTORS ONLY

Anthropology, like individual cultures, is a complex, interrelated system of meaning with different levels of understanding and multiple alternative interpretations. Addressing any particular ethnographic fact, heuristic theory, mode of analysis, field work methodology, or epistemological presumption implies reference to other facts, theories, modes, methodologies, and presumptions and leads one up and down to different levels of understanding and to other interpretations. The same is true of paleoanthropology, with its additional element of attempting to find and evaluate evidence in the past without being able to see events as they occur, revisit data for verification, or even talk with people.

There is no ideal way to introduce anthropology to students. Wherever we start, we must fan out in all directions, reach up and down, make connections, and survey the landscape. Whatever we start with, we must end up someplace else. If we begin with the very general, we must proceed to the particular; if we begin with the particular, we must advance to the general. We can start with individual ethnographies but will eventually get to a discussion of religion, economy, and kinship; we can begin with religion and politics but end with hunters and cultivators. We can discuss Old World and New World pyramids in terms of architectural similarities but end up discussing differences of function; we can begin comparing primate femurs and end up with a discussion of different locomotor patterns and why hominid bipedalism evolved.

So wherever we begin, whatever we begin to teach our students about anthropology, there are 23 or 230 other places we are not teaching about that are implied in what we are saying or that are necessary to conceptualize it. Of course we cannot speak about everything at once. We must start at one point and proceed around the great circle of anthropology. And our students must learn about one thing at a time, initially oblivious to its connections with all of the rest. This is inevitable and cannot be avoided.

However, to paraphrase John Dewey, this anthropological reality is not a problem because there is no solution to it. But this challenge is the *raison d'être* for *Thinking Anthropologically*. This readily available supplementary text provides overviews of major spheres in anthropology. In easy-to-read prose aimed at introductory-level students, this collection of essays offers accounts of the general frameworks that underlie anthropology:

> Chapter 2: **"What Anthropologists Look For: Patterns."** What are anthropologists looking for, and what counts as anthropological knowledge?
>
> Chapter 3: **"Thinking Holistically."** What are the different subdivisions of anthropology, and how do their interrelationships contribute to anthropological knowledge and thinking?
>
> Chapter 4: **"Thinking Theoretically."** What is theory, and what part does it play in anthropology?
>
> Chapter 5: **"Using Science to Think Anthropologically."** What is science, and how can it be used in anthropology?
>
> Chapter 6: **"Thinking about Change: Biological Evolution, Culture Change, and the Importance of Scale."** How can we think about and understand change?
>
> Chapter 7: **"Why Do Anthropological Experts Disagree?"** Why do anthropologists disagree about evidence and interpretations?
>
> Chapter 8: **"Thinking and Acting Ethically in Anthropology."** What does ethics have to do with anthropology, and why should we be concerned about ethics anyhow?
>
> Chapter 9: **"Applying Anthropological Knowledge."** How is anthropological knowledge used in the real world?
>
> Chapter 10: **"How to Take Anthropology Tests."** How can students take anthropology tests and do well?

The discussions in *Thinking Anthropologically* provide an overview of anthropological thinking, helping students follow the material you are covering in your teaching and the substantive content in the main text or case studies that you use. *Thinking Anthropologically* relieves the introductory instructor of the need to cover these background frameworks while attempting to impart knowledge in the classroom. It gives students a ready reference in the areas that are likely to puzzle them.

Although instructors can assign individual chapters or the entire primer, as needed, we envision *Thinking Anthropologically* as a basic student aid in introductory courses. If your students learn to think anthropologically early on, they will better understand you and the major text you use, they will do better in the course, and they will appreciate anthropology more. We suggest assigning the book for the first week of class.

Finally, we ask you not only to assign this volume to your students but also to help us improve it. Which chapters were the most useful and which the least useful? Were there problems with individual chapters? Which other topics would you and your students like covered in a new edition? Please let us know. You can find both Philip Carl Salzman and Patricia Rice and our e-mail addresses in the American Anthropological Association Guide, available through www.aaanet.org. We would like to hear what you think.

# What Anthropologists
# Look For: Patterns

PHILIP CARL SALZMAN, *McGill University*

When anthropologists study people, what are they looking for? What do they want to know, and how do they know when they know something? When you study people and peoples, and cultures and societies, what should you be looking for?

Archaeologists examine the remains of past cultures by sorting through pot shards, stone implements, and bones. They are looking for patterns of tool use, site occupation, and ritual activity. Physical and biological anthropologists study the human body, its variations, and commonalities within and between populations. They are looking for patterns of interaction between environments and genetic populations and between populations. Linguists focus on language as a coherent system and as an integral part of culture and society. They are looking for patterns of language commonality or variation in relation to social life and cultural orientations. Sociocultural anthropologists talk to people about their ideas and values, observe people as they go about their lives, and monitor their activities. They are looking for patterns in belief and value, in the conjunction of ideas and actions, and in the relationship between different practices and institutions.

What would you be looking for if you were faced with an opportunity like the one I had doing my first ethnographic field research? I remember driving slowly across the desert in Baluchistan, in southeastern Iran, dodging the small sand dunes as our Land Rover approached a line of black goat hair tents, the home of a herding group of Baluchi tribal nomads. We were approached by a dignified, bearded man of middle age wearing a turban, baggy trousers, and a long shirt hanging to his knees. My wife and I waited while our companion, the charming brother of the tribal chief, got out to explain to this amazed camp headman that we wanted to live with him and his community. Soon thereafter, we were setting up our baby blue canvas exoskeleton tent (totally unsuitable for local conditions, as it turned out) near the tent of the headman, Jafar. Once our household was set up and we had begun to figure out how to live in a tent in the desert, I turned my attention to research.

One main thing I wanted to know was how these Baluchi nomads made a living amid the sand dunes. Of course, I was not starting from zero, from complete ignorance, because I had read about Middle Eastern and Iranian nomads and had some idea what I was likely to find in Baluchistan. So I was not alone in my research; I relied on anthropological ideas and ethnographic information provided by anthropologists (and historians and travelers) who had thought about these problems and done research before me. (Anthropology is a collective project in other, parallel ways: Educational institutions train new anthropologists and provide jobs; public and private funding agencies provide the money needed for research.)

## PATTERNS IN MAKING A LIVING

Middle Eastern nomads as we know them from previous studies done in the twentieth century, made a living (at least partly) by raising livestock: sheep, goats, and camels. Some, such as the Rwala Bedouin (Lancaster 1997) of northern Arabia, raised mainly camels; some, such as the Basseri of southwestern Iran (Barth 1961), raised mainly sheep; the Baluchi nomads, as I (Salzman 2000) discovered in the course of my research, raised mainly goats but sheep also (two goats for each sheep) and had a small number of camels.

This is our first example of what anthropologists look for: **patterns in the life of a human population or group. Pattern** in anthropology and social science more generally means a repetition of a social or cultural phenomenon—a belief, a practice, a custom, an institution—over space or time. For example, that Middle Eastern nomads raised livestock (as distinct from some nomads elsewhere, who hunt for a living) on natural pasture (pastoralism) is a pattern; that different groups of nomads raised different animal species (or in markedly different ratios) is another pattern.

What about nomadism? Why did these nomads move their households and community groups regularly? Mainly they moved to accommodate their livestock; they moved to find the best pasture and water for their animals and to avoid disease, predators, and enemies. But not all nomads followed the same **pattern of migration.** The Basseri (Barth 1961) migrated in a fairly regular way between mountain summer pastures and lowland winter pastures. In contrast, the Baluch (Salzman 2000) moved first one way and then another, in an irregular fashion, the pattern changing each year. What was predictable about the Baluchi migration pattern was that it was unpredictable. So different nomadic groups had different migration patterns.

The patterns we have discussed so far are **descriptive** in that they report a characteristic of a particular population or group. When I say "they mostly had camels," that is a descriptive pattern of **central tendency,** a kind of average. It tells you the main thing but not everything. When I say, "they had a 2:1 ratio of goats to sheep and some camels as well," the descriptive pattern is one of **distribution,** indicating not only the main thing but the more minor things as well.

Descriptive patterns are answers to the question "What is present here?" But anthropologists also ask "Why is this pattern present here?" Another kind of pattern, **associational patterns,** which show how some characteristics are associated with other characteristics, are (at least partial) answers to the "Why?" question.

For example, if we investigate why some Middle Eastern nomads herded sheep, some herded goats, and others herded camels, we will discover that there is an association between the kind of livestock herded and the environment, particularly the climate. The nomads who herded mainly sheep lived in more humid environments (10 or more inches of rainfall), whereas those who herded mainly goats lived in arid environments (5 inches of rain a year), and those who herded mainly camels lived in very arid environments (less than 3 inches of a rain a year).

Similarly, migration patterns are also associated with aridity. Nomads such as the Basseri, who migrated regularly and predictably between summer and winter pastures seasonally, lived in more humid environments, whereas nomads such as the Rwala Bedouin and the Baluch, who lived in more arid environments, followed erratic and irregular migration patterns to find pasture and water wherever it was available. This relationship between migration and climate, like the relationship between livestock species and climate, is an associational pattern, which shows that certain characteristics go together, or are correlated.

Another aspect of the Baluchi nomadic economy quickly caught my attention. I went to Baluchistan hoping to study nomads who did nothing but raise livestock, who were called "pure" nomads by some anthropologists. When I confided this to the tribal chief, he appeared to have no idea what I was talking about. The reason was that all Baluchi nomads were involved in several different sectors of production. Yes, Baluchi men raised livestock, but they also cultivated date palms, engaged in small-scale grain cultivation, occasionally hunted and gathered, and, in the past, engaged in predatory raiding of peasants and caravans, but more recently many left the tribal territory to work for money or engage in trade. We can sum up this descriptive pattern by saying that the Baluchi economy was not specialized, focused on one product, but was rather mixed or multiresource, distributed among several spheres of production.

Why did some nomads, such as the Rwala Bedouin and the Basseri, specialize in economic production, putting most of their efforts into their livestock, whereas other nomads, such as the Baluch and the Nuer (Evans-Pritchard 1940) of the southern Sudan, were committed to cultivating, raiding, trading, or, in the case of the Nuer, who raised cattle in a very humid environment, fishing. Are specialized livestock breeding and mixed or multiresource production associated with different circumstances?

In general, nomads who had multiresource economies had them because of their consumption practices: they were subsistence oriented, producing goods for their own consumption. For this reason, they had to produce a range of products—milk, meat, wool, hair, leather, but also grain, dates, green vegetables, and, where applicable, fish—to provide a full diet and raw materials for what they need to make, such as goat hair for tents and wool for clothes and luggage bags. The Baluch and Nuer lived on what they produced, so they had to produce everything they needed.

In contrast, nomadic peoples who had specialized economies had them because they were market oriented, planned to sell their livestock in the market and to purchase whatever consumption goods they needed in the market. While the Rwala were herding their camels deep in the empty deserts of northern Arabia they were thinking about the urban markets that would buy their camels to supply the caravan trade. Similarly, the Basseri trekking with their sheep through the high Zagros mountains of Iran were planning to sell them in the bazaar of the garden city of Shiraz and buy clothes, grain, dried vegetables, tea, and sugar there.

The associational pattern we have identified here is that nomads specialized in pastoral production of livestock when they could sell animals in the marketplace and could buy their consumption goods with the money they received, whereas nomads who relied on what they produced for consumption had multiresource economies to provide them with the necessary range of products.

The nomadic, pastoral, multiresource **pattern of land use** that I saw when I was doing research in Baluchistan had been present for at least 100 years. But was it always the pattern of land use in that part of Baluchistan? This question can be answered only through evidence about what happened in the past and through time. In the absence of accessible historical records, we turn to anthropological archaeologists to answer this question. Archaeologists examine the physical remains of the past to discover patterns existing in different periods. An archaeological survey of the area of Baluchistan I studied shows impressive remains from the past, remains that demonstrate definitively that in the past a totally different pattern of land use was dominant.

Across today's desert landscape are seen what might look like rows of bomb craters: a line of holes each surrounded by a rim of soil. But these are the surface manifestations of *qanat,* underground water tunnels for irrigation. Each hole and rim mark the place where soil was removed to make the tunnel and where workers entered the tunnel to maintain it. *Qanat,* sometimes 10 or more kilometers long, begin at a point where the mother well taps the water table at an altitude higher than the place to be irrigated, and gravity brings the water downhill until it comes to the surface at the irrigation site.

The archaeological survey mentioned earlier, finding 73 *qanat* remains, shows that prior to the last century of nomadic land use, irrigation agriculture was dominant in this region. Irrigation agriculture requires the ongoing presence of cultivators to distribute the water to the crops in a precise and systematic fashion. To do this, and to protect the crops, the cultivators would have had to be mainly sedentary. Thus, thanks to archaeological analysis, we now know that the pattern of land use in this area of Baluchistan has changed markedly over time. The shift from irrigation agriculture to nomadic pastoralism and multiresource exploitation identifies an important **historical pattern** for this region.

## PATTERNS IN MARRIAGE, FAMILY, AND COMMUNITY

Among the Baluchi nomads, the family was more important than in industrial America and Europe. The reason for this is clear: families and their associated households not only provided a residence, a place for the consumption of food, biological reproduction, and the socialization and enculturation of children, but also were the unit of economic production, in which all the things people needed were produced.

A new family and a new household were formed by marriage, and the position of that family among others was determined by the kinship ties of each partner to his or her parents, siblings, and other relatives. Marriages, especially first marriages, usually were arranged by parents, with the consent of the engaged couple. Whom did the Baluchi nomads marry?

As in much of the Middle East, Baluchi nomads prefered to marry close relatives. "Marry a cousin and you know what you are getting," they told me. And when they say "what you are getting," they were considering not only the spouse, whose character and abilities were well understood, but also parents-in-law, brothers-in-law, and all relatives by marriage, with whom one would be closely involved. The Baluch prefered patrilateral, parallel cousin marriage, that is, marriage to one's father's brother's children. Why did the Baluch and other Middle Eastern nomads favor the father's brother's children over the mother's brother's or father's sister's children? The reason for this is clear: Baluchi nomads, like all other Middle Eastern nomads, reckoned descent through the male line and organized important defense and cooperation groups in terms of descent through a common male ancestor. By marrying your father's brother's child, you would be certain of marrying a member of your own defense group within which solidarity and support were expected. Your in-laws would be members of your defense group. Such marriages thus led to maximum solidarity in both the family and the defense group.

The preference that one marry close, and marry close patrilineal kin if possible, is a descriptive pattern, like specializing in goats. But whereas the animals one specializes in are described by a **statistical pattern,** the injunction to marry close is a **normative pattern** because it is felt to be the right thing to do and forms a rule of behavior. Baluch would not say you are wrong to specialize in sheep (although they might say you were unwise), but they would say you are wrong for disdaining close marriages and seeking distant ones. But even the normative pattern of marriage alliance is a **preferential** normative pattern, in that it is not obligatory. What if one looked to marry close, but there were no potential partners because everyone close and unmarried was too young or too old? Or maybe one's father did not have a brother, or his brother did not have a child of the appropriate gender or age. In such a case, marrying a more distant person would not be condemned. (The distance can be smoothed over semantically by referring to a second, third, or fourth cousin in a "classificatory" fashion as "my cousin" or "my father's brother's child" even though he or she is really one's father's father's brother's son's child.)

Such preferential normative patterns can be distinguished from **mandatory** or obligatory normative patterns, such as taking care of your children and not abusing your spouse. These are strict rules, and breaking them could not be justified; condemnation by public opinion would have been swift and sure. Another mandatory rule was that if a member of your lineage defense group was being attacked, you must go and defend that person as if you yourself were being attacked. Anthropologists call this rule collective responsibility, in which each member is obliged to act with total solidarity with all of the others, in the spirit of "all for one and one for all." (The North Atlantic Treaty Organization, NATO, has a similar rule, in which an attack on one is to be regarded as an attack on all.)

But normative rules are one thing, and humans' actions often are another thing. American parents commonly impose rules for their children against smoking, drinking, driving fast, and premarital intimacies. Notwithstanding the mandatory nature of these norms, young people often conduct their lives beyond the sight of their parents with disregard for such rules. Therefore, in addition to knowing the normative pattern, we need to look at the statistical or behavioral pattern as well, so that we can see how many people follow the rule and how many do not follow it. In Middle Eastern societies, although most people married not-too-distant relatives, only about 10 percent of marriages were between real patrilateral, parallel cousins; in communities with the best record, no more than half achieved this ideal (Barth 1954).

Similarly with mandatory normative patterns, the statistical pattern of actual behavior commonly shows a few people who violate the norm, who do not turn up to help their lineage mates, who do beat their wives, who do not take care of their children. In response to these violations the community generally takes some punitive measures, from verbal condemnation, through withdrawal of support, to expulsion. Anthropologists view these punitive measures as part of the **pattern of social control** through which a population maintains a set of rules and standards and thus a particular, cultural way of doing things.

When I describe the Middle Eastern marriage pattern, students often say, "Yikes! Marry my cousin? No way!" And then they ask whether Middle Easterners have deformities from marrying their cousins. This question takes us into the realm of biological anthropology. Framed more generally, the question is about an associational pattern: are marriages between close relatives associated with biological deformities or other negative consequences? In general, we can say that marriage between relatives is associated with deleterious effects only when a particular **genetic pattern** is present: a deleterious, recessive gene. In this case, the negative characteristic appears only at the phenotype (or external, bodily) level when two individuals, both with the recessive gene, contribute that gene to offspring. When such a deleterious recessive gene is present in a family line, the chances of two recessive genes coming together is greater if people are marrying close relatives. If both partners carry the recessive gene, 25 percent of their offspring will show the deleterious effect. Whether a given population increases the risk of negative consequences from marriage with relatives depends on their genetic pattern. (Of course, there may be social benefits from marriage with relatives that might outweigh such biological risks, should they exist.)

## PATTERNS IN SOCIAL CONTROL AND POLITICS

Among the nomadic tribes of Baluchistan, security and defense were the responsibility of corporate lineage groups, groups defined by common descent through the male line. These lineage groups did not exist all of the time, for two reasons.

First, each tribesman and tribeswoman belonged to lineages of different sizes, depending on which ancestor one was counting from. A grandfather was the founder of a small microlineage, a great-grandfather was the founder of a larger minor lineage, and a great-great-grandfather was the founder of a fairly large medium lineage, and so on up to tribal sections, whole tribes, and sometimes tribal confederacies. However, whether the members of a lineage were called together to form an action group for defense depended on circumstances, particularly a threat to life or property. Which lineage became relevant at a particular moment and became activated, which lineage a tribesman thought about and counted himself a member of, depended on the opposing group threatening one's security. If a conflict broke out between close relatives, then each would gather the members of his microlineage together to help him. If those in conflict were distant genealogically, then they would call on their medium or macrolineages to support them. So whether a given Baluch thought of himself as a member of the Shadi Hanzai microlineage or a member of the Soherabzai macrolineage depended on the circumstances, specifically who his opponent was. Anthropologists call such groups contingent groups in that they are called into existence and action only in response to certain circumstances, or contingencies.

The second reason that these defense groups did not exist all of the time was that people did not engage in security and defensive activities all of the time. Unlike our police officers, soldiers, and firefighters, who put on their uniforms and go to work each day, all men in a Baluchi tribe are members of lineage defense groups at the same time as they are herders, cultivators, traders, and nomads. Members of a lineage defense group live in different residential communities. So when defense matters arise, lineage members must be activated; the Baluch must drop whatever they are doing and come together to decide what actions to take.

The pattern of contingency (or its opposite, permanence) in action groups can be called a **meta-pattern** in that it applies to many specific descriptive patterns. Meta-patterns can also be found in historical and prehistorical patterns, that is, over time, as the following example indicates.

Among the Baluchi tribes and elsewhere, existing social and cultural patterns are not all of equal strength: some are strongly manifest whereas others are weaker, or latent. On a day-to-day basis in Baluchistan, people may be focusing on raising their livestock and growing their crops, not thinking about security and defense. At this moment, defense groups are latent. When a serious conflict arises, people organize into defense groups, which then become manifest. This is what is meant by *contingent pattern*.

We see a similar latent/manifest alternation in the two main Baluchi political institutions, the lineages and the tribal chiefship. Lineages come to the fore as opponents during conflict; the tribal chief comes to the fore as a mediator stressing peace and trying to reestablish unity.

This contingency can also exist over long periods of time, historical time. During periods of strife, lineage affiliation and defense groups are manifest and central. During such times, other foci, such as religion, tend to recede and weaken. But during periods of peace, religion, in the Baluch case Sunni Islam, can be activated as a major concern and focus of activity. In this way, there can be an alternation over time, with religion strongly manifest and lineage defense groups latent for a period, whereas in another period lineage defense groups are strongly manifest and religion weak and latent.

To take another example, during periods of political independence, Baluchi tribesmen were active and enthusiastic predatory raiders, robbing caravans and distant villages. Once conquered and encapsulated by the Iranian state in 1935, the tribesmen turned their energies and creativity to (among other things) expanding their limited agricultural cultivation. Even irrigation technology, long out of use in the region, was reactivated. This meta-pattern of alternation through prehistoric and historical time is widespread and can be seen in many specific patterns.

## CONCLUSION

What anthropologists look for in studying culture and society is **patterns in the life of a human population or group.** This includes, among many others, patterns of land use, patterns of movement, production patterns, marriage patterns, and defense cooperation patterns.

One main kind of pattern that anthropologists seek, especially in ethnographic field research, is **descriptive patterns** that convey many important characteristics of the particular society and culture being studied. Descriptive patterns can report a **central tendency,** one or another form of average (for example, Baluchi nomadic households contain on average 6.3 individuals); alternatively, a **distributional pattern** reports the range of cases (for example, Baluchi nomadic households range from 2 to 13 individuals, with the second and third quartiles ranging from 4.6 to 7.2 individuals).

One kind of descriptive pattern is a **historical pattern** that reports changes in human activity, such as in land use pattern, over time. One **meta-pattern** that we have seen is the alternation of specific cultural patterns through time (such as lineage and chiefly dominance, or conflict and religion in Baluchistan) in both short-term and long, historical cycles.

The number of individuals in a household is a **statistical pattern** or **behavioral pattern,** as is the percentage of people praying every day or the number who prefer to herd sheep rather than goats. Another kind of pattern is the **normative pattern,** a rule or moral obligation, such as helping lineage mates among the Baluch or abstaining from sexual relations outside of marriage. Normative patterns can be **preferential** in that the rule is regarded as a good thing to follow (such as marrying a close relative) or **mandatory** (such as joining with lineage mates to take vengeance on attackers from another lineage).

When we are examining the relationship between two descriptive patterns, we might discover an **associational pattern** that illustrates that two descriptive patterns are co-related or correlated with one another and tend to appear together. Examples include the association between regular migration patterns and regular, predictable climates, and between irregular migration patterns and irregular, unpredictable climates, and the association between subsistence-oriented production and multiresource economies, and between market-oriented production and specialized economies.

## REFERENCES

BARTH, FREDRIK
  1954. "Father's Brother's Daughter Marriage in Kurdistan." *Southwestern Journal of Anthropology* 10:164–71.
  1961. *Nomads of South Persia.* Oslo: Oslo University Press.
EVANS-PRITCHARD E. E.
  1940. *The Nuer.* Oxford: The Clarendon Press.
LANCASTER, WILLIAM
  1997. *The Rwala Bedouin Today* (2nd edition). Prospect Heights, IL: Waveland.
SALZMAN, PHILIP CARL
  2000. *Black Tents of Baluchistan.* Washington, DC: Smithsonian Institution Press.

# Thinking Holistically

HOLLY PETERS-GOLDEN, *University of Michigan*

Whether the course you are taking is an introductory anthropology class address-ing all of the subdisciplines (biological anthropology, cultural anthropology, archaeology, and linguistic anthropology) or one that focuses on one of these fields, chances are you will begin with a discussion of holism. Holism is a central defining concept in anthropology, one that sets it apart from other disciplines that study humanity. What is holism? Why is it such a critical feature of anthropol-ogy? Finally, why do anthropologists think holistically?

When used in a general sense, holism might be most familiarly represented by the expression "the whole is greater than the sum of its parts." In adding up all the particulars, the end result is something more than–and different from–those constituent elements. This is true for an individual human being, who is certainly more than the sum of biological traits and cultural knowledge; it is also true for an entire society, which is not merely a collection of individual members (Schultz and Lavenda 1998).

The **holistic perspective in anthropology** tries to take into consideration all aspects of human life, as found throughout time and across space. Holism is the "study of the whole of the human condition: past, present, and future; biology, sci-ence, language, and culture" (Kottak 2002). Through cross-cultural comparative studies, we can recognize both the great diversity between peoples as well as the human characteristics that unite us all. Anthropologists don't generalize about "human nature" or "the way people are" without taking into consideration a wide range of different societies. However, it is not sufficient merely to cast a wide enough net to capture all the varied features of human life. We cannot accurately represent anthropology by defining it as being made up of biological, cultural, linguistic, and archaeological aspects, lined up side by side. It is the ways in which all these aspects are integrated, the elegant ways in which they influence one another, that exemplifies anthropology's holistic perspective.

Speaking literally, holism is something of an ideal. Whatever anthropology's best intentions, it is impossible to know everything about all of humanity. The depth and breadth of human existence are vast. Human beings and their cultures are complex and changing; we are continually learning new facts and revising old assumptions. Yet anthropology strives to maintain the holistic perspective on several levels, recognizing that each part of culture is connected to and influenced by the other parts and by the whole, that the past is connected to the present (and the future), and that each of the four subdisciplines is inextricably bound to the others.

The essence of thinking anthropologically is 'thinking holistically.' What follows in this chapter are examples of holism, both between the subdisciplines and within each subdicipline, designed to help you begin to recognize the process of asking questions, making comparisons, weighing alternatives, and looking at the study of humankind the way anthropologists do: holistically.

## HOLISM: CONNECTIONS WITHIN CULTURES

The concept of culture is central to anthropology and central to the holistic perspective. Culture, the learned beliefs and behaviors characteristic of a particular group, can provide the organizing framework for demonstrating the ways in which the varied aspects of human life—art, politics, religion, marriage, family, economics, and medicine, to name a few—are **interdependent.** The economic system of a society influences the meaning of a marriage alliance; food production is tied to political systems. Gender roles can vary in relation to economic systems; religious rituals may serve environmental ends. Art can reflect social oppression; illness beliefs can grow out of gender stereotypes. The holistic perspective begins with the assumption that cultures are **integrated systems** that contain recognizable patterns of belief and behavior, threads woven into a larger fabric of meaning and practice. However, culture is not a restrictive mandate to be followed blindly, nor is it one rigid set of rules without alternatives. People often challenge cultural rules and negotiate change in an active, creative way.

On a more complex level, the imbalance of birth rates between boys and girls in parts of rural China provides a powerful example of the **interrelationship** of politics, economics, kinship, law, family structure, and medical technology. Decades ago, in an attempt to stem overpopulation, the Chinese government instituted a policy that mandated no more than one child per couple; in some parts of the country, a second child is permitted if the first child is a girl. Those who violate this rule are subject to fines. Some wealthy people are able to shoulder the economic burden of stiff fines, but most rural villagers cannot. In much of rural China, daughters move at marriage to live with their husband's family, and it is sons on whom the financial security of the family rests. Moreover, in the absence of government health care, elderly parents depend on sons to care for them in their old age. Recently, inexpensive prenatal scans have become available to pregnant villagers, and despite laws against such screening, they are used to determine the sex of a fetus, with the result that females are sometimes aborted. Recent census data show that the worldwide average birth ratio is 106 boys to 100 girls, whereas in 2000, China's national average was 117 boys to 100 girls; in some parts of the countryside, the ratio was 144:100. The marital consequences of China's "missing girls" are already in evidence, with reports of women being abducted and sold to men who cannot find wives, seen by the villagers as a disastrous economic and cultural situation (Eckholm 2002). Alarmed by the selective abortion of females, Chinese officials and scholars have recognized the ways many aspects of rural village life—government mandates, poverty, gaps in health care, gender bias, and many others—act together, and the government has begun to mount programs to address the problem holistically, knowing that one cultural phenomenon will affect the others.

## HOLISM: CONNECTIONS ACROSS THE FOUR FIELDS

Despite the widely shared holistic perspective that guides anthropologists to examine the whole range of human life, the discipline of anthropology is generally divided into four areas of study: cultural anthropology, biological anthropology, archaeology, and linguistic anthropology. However, each subfield illuminates related issues in the others.

The beginnings of American anthropology, roughly 100 years ago, grew out of an interest in the history and culture of the peoples native to North America. The questions early anthropologists asked about the diverse indigenous peoples of North America spanned what we now identify as the four fields or subdiscipines. Native Americans spoke different languages, had different social structures and different customs in general, differed in physical appearance, and perhaps had different origins. Once the reservation system was in place, it was generally feared that these cultures would disappear, spurring American anthropologists to do all they could to preserve at least a record of as much as possible. Anthropologists attempted to study every aspect of native language, culture, artifacts, and physical features (Bourguignon 1996). Thus, the holistic perspective in America is rooted in the very inception of the discipline.

Perhaps the best way to demonstrate the principle of holism across the discipline of anthropology is to examine the ways in which these four areas of inquiry are interconnected.

### Archaeology Connects

When students think of **archaeology,** what often comes to mind are things rather than people: shards of pottery, bits of animal bones, and stones shaped into weapons and tools. A cultural anthropologist can ask questions of a group of people to learn about their culture, but how can an archaeologist get answers to questions about the past? Rather than **observe** behavior the way ethnographers (cultural anthropologists) do, archaeologists **reconstruct** behavior through their study of material remains. The grandest of pyramids and the smallest grain of fossilized pollen can "speak" to an archaeologist. In fact, the archaeological record can offer at least a partial understanding of peoples and their cultures with whom it is impossible to talk. Cultural anthropologists provide a wealth of information about people all over the world, but their study of society and culture generally cannot reach back beyond several hundred years. Archaeology can reveal ways of life that are no longer observable and provide an understanding of long-term cultural change (Jolly and White 1995). Here, the link is between the past and the present as well as between two anthropological subfields.

The material remains that have been left behind can illuminate cultural patterns in the past, but are they holistic patterns? Archaeologists can determine whether groups of people were food gatherers or food cultivators and whether the animals they consumed were wild or domesticated, thereby providing insights into ancient economies. By examining artifacts—materials that people have made or modified in some way—we may learn about many aspects of prehistoric life. Discerning what prehistoric peoples ate may seem unimportant, but as archaeologist Robert Ehrenreich (1996) points out, myriad other questions and issues arise out of inquiry into diet. For example, how did diet change over time, and why? What role did food play in population size? How was food secured and prepared, and by whom? What sort of rituals or aesthetics surrounded food? How might diet provide information about social organization, beliefs about health, prestige, celebration, or division of labor? This suggests that archaeologists do seek holistic patterns because diet appears to have been closely related to social organization, social roles, art, ritual, and economics in the past just as it is in the present.

Consider the cultural information archaeologists can provide through just one kind of artifact: potsherds, or fragments of pottery. The quantity of pottery bits found at a site might indicate the population size. Materials used in making pottery but not found locally point toward trading activities. At different sites, the discovery of pots that are similar in various features may be a result of a host of cultural connections (Kottak 2002). Archaeologists contribute to our understanding of ecology, the ways states and cities arise, economic and social organization, and even gender roles. In addition to contributions to our understanding of prehistory, archaeologists also provide insights into recent history and modern peoples. For example, archaeologists excavating sites in the American South are reconstructing the lifeways of eighteenth-century slaves transported from Africa to work on plantations. Previously, information about the diet, clothing, and possessions of slave families was gathered through the manifests of their owners. Written records kept by plantation owners detailed meals and material goods furnished to slaves; the "ethnographic record" was akin to the inventory in a store. The list of foods provided for slaves was assumed to be an accurate representation of foods the slaves ate; clothing and household items given to them were recorded as their possessions. However, archaeological excavation of the slave quarters shows an entirely different, very rich culture. Bones of small game that were hunted on a regular basis are evidence of a supplemented diet; pottery and baskets were fashioned for decoration and utility. Also unearthed were game pieces such as homemade dominoes and a variety of musical instruments. The material remains archaeologists find can rewrite ethnography.

In its discovery and interpretation of past environments and inhabitants, archaeology is also connected to biological anthropology. Archaeologists and biological anthropologists share many of the same concepts and techniques in their mutual study of humanity's past (Schultz and Lavenda 1998). Biological anthropologists who study the fossil record of human evolution work closely with archaeologists to reveal a picture of the human past that is both biological and cultural. For example, the position of Neandertal in our human ancestry is contentious at best and probably will continue to be so in the future. (See Chapter 7 for a discussion of the roots of this controversy.) Bioanthropologists compare populations in existence before and particularly after Neandertals existed in Europe and the Near East to assess the possibility of evolutionary connections; archaeologists compare artifacts before and after Neandertal in the same areas to assess the possibility of cultural connections between populations that would show up in artifact similarities. We will never be able to conclude whether Neandertal had anything to do with our ancestry unless we look at both the biology and culture of that population and the modern one that succeeded it. If the DNA and artifact clusters of the two groups are too different to conclude interconnections, then we will probably conclude that Neandertal had nothing to do with modern human ancestry. If we find biological traits evolving during Neandertal times that carry over into earliest populations of modern humans and cultural traditions that both populations share, then we will probably conclude that Neandertal did have something to do with our past. At the moment, there is no consensus about this question except that it is a biocultural question with a biocultural answer.

Although language doesn't fossilize, archaeological evidence can still shed some light on this topic. Increasing complexity in tools and other artifacts corresponds with increasing brain complexity, one part of which is the development of language and speech. In the argument about when complex language originated, some say it was a result of a great increase in cultural abilities. Other researchers look at cultural accomplishments documented in the archaeological record, including bone tools, complex stone tool traditions, cave art, and burials, and ask whether they would all be possible without language already being in place. One interesting experiment attempted to show when speech might have been necessary in tool manufacturing. An expert in flint tool making (called flint knapping) taught a group of ten volunteers how to make handaxes by imitation; the students simply did exactly what the expert did, and they were all successful in making a simple flint handaxe, the most common large tool manufactured between 2.6 million years ago and about 40 thousand years ago. They could also make flake tools with retouched edges by watching the instructor hit the edge of the flake with his antler hammer. But the students were totally unsuccessful at making blade tools using only imitation. Blade tool manufacture, which became the norm starting about 40 thousand years ago, apparently demands oral instruction for success (Bernard 1980).

## Linguistic Anthropology Connects

Despite the fact that we do not know when our human ancestors began to **speak,** we do know that **language** is central to being human. (Note that the terms *language* and *speech* are different in that language is not necessarily oral, whereas speech is, but we will use the terms interchangeably.) The reach of linguistic anthropology, the study of language in its cultural context, extends across time and place and also extends to the other fields of anthropology. A central theme in holistic anthropology is the recognition of both the diversity of humanity and the commonalities that underpin it. Language is a vehicle for demonstrating at the same time the universal and the particular in human life: all humans share the capacity for language, but there is a rich diversity in the several thousand languages about which we have data. This linguistic diversity correlates with cultural diversity (Hickerson 1997).

Language is at the heart of the way we engage with each other and with the world around us. Through language, children learn the intricacies of their culture to become members of their society. In learning a group's language, we learn more than words, grammar, and pronunciation; we learn about the culture in which that language is used. The centrality of this tenet is reflected in the fact that cultural anthropologists conduct their field work in the language of the people among whom they are working. Early linguistic anthropologist Edward Sapir wrote in 1912, "The worlds in which different societies live are distinct worlds, not merely the same world with different labels attached" (as quoted by Bonvillain 1997:49).

As the vehicle through which we think, communicate, and organize our beliefs about the way the world works, language can provide insights into culture. Linguistic anthropologists study a variety of features of language, such as structure, history, sound, change, meaning, acquisition, and use. Each of these can illuminate assumptions, values, and interests of the wider culture in which the language is found. For example, language can reveal social inequality through hierarchical differences in terms of address, greetings, pronouns, and kinship terms. Speakers of a language can convey distance, solidarity, respect, collegiality, superiority, class, and power by choosing from among various titles, names, and expressions. Japanese society is stratified in terms of class, gender, and age, with deference shown to wealthy people and those in high-status jobs, to men, and to the elderly. Many features of the Japanese language reflect these differences in status, with choice of words, titles, grammatical constructions, and tone directed by the relative rank of those conversing (Bonvillain 1997).

By comparing the speech of men and women in a variety of social settings, linguistic anthropologists have demonstrated numerous differences in language use. Men and women have been shown to use different vocabularies, styles of speech, grammar, and tone. Gendered patterns of speech reflect social roles of women and men, exemplifying "proper" behavior as well as defining the realms in which they are expected to have knowledge.

The lexicon of a language—its inventory of words—is another connection between language and culture. The stock of words exemplifies what is important to a group. Think of the explosion of terms and expressions linked to computers and cyberspace that has occurred in recent years. Foragers and horticulturalists can name far more plants than people in industrial societies; residents of the Arctic have words to describe variations in ice and snow that people in temperate climates could never distinguish (Kottak 2002). Similar examples can be found in sports terms, colors, foods, types of animals, and more: Serena Nanda and Rich Warms (1998) report that residents of Munich, Germany have more than seventy words to describe the color, strength, carbonation, and other qualities of beer.

Language can be a powerful tool for both domination and resistance. Throughout history, people have felt and expressed their identity through language. Its importance is demonstrated by the fact that political and social oppression often includes the mandate that a group give up its own language. Resistance to such an edict is a vehicle for rebellion and sometimes takes very clever form: when Chinese authorities attempted to prevent the Hmong ethnic minority from speaking their own language, Hmong women, who are renowned textile artists, devised a pictorial code that they appliquéd to their skirts, sending messages to one another and making fun of their oppressors (Willcox 1986).

The link between language and culture may be obvious, but the study of language is relevant to archaeology and biological anthropology as well. Historical linguistics studies the development and change of language over time. Changes, differences, and similarities across languages can indicate common origins as well as contact through marriage, trade relations, and even war. Historical linguists have worked with archaeologists to trace the spread of particular technologies and material culture by linking them to the spread of language (Scupin and DeCorse 2001).

Language and human origins have a connection that is basic to anthropology: our elaboration of and dependence on language often is cited as one of the defining features that makes us human. Biological anthropologists are interested in the development and evolution of the capacities for human language in the brain and speech via the vocal anatomy. Language is a bridge between the biological and cultural aspects of humanity, demonstrating their interconnectedness.

In addition to investigating the beginnings of language in humans, biological anthropologists compare communication systems among humans and nonhuman primates. There is much controversy over the interpretation of results of studies teaching apes to use sign language and other forms of symbolic communication. However, it seems clear that in many aspects the differences between humans and apes are not as great as was previously believed. Given that humans and apes share common ancestry, when did our communicative abilities begin to differ (Relethford 2000)? When did we begin to speak?

### Biological Anthropology Connects

Whereas some anthropologists are concerned primarily with cultural beliefs and practices and others focus on **biological evolution** and **modern human variation,** all anthropologists would agree that the essence of being human is grounded in the interconnection of biology and culture. We are biological organisms, with both needs and limitations dictated by that nature. But we are cultural beings as well, and it is our ability to learn and our capacity for culture that set us apart from other animals. Human biology and human culture are engaged in an elegant dance that has spanned all the times and all the places of human existence. The transformative interaction of biology and culture sometimes is demonstrated by referring to humankind as biocultural.

As we examine the evolution of humanity, we see biological and cultural changes often working together. It was the combination of advances in both biology and culture that allowed us to continue to evolve and thrive. Anatomical changes in locomotion allowed early humans to travel greater distances to gather and hunt more efficiently. More sophisticated tool kits resulted in further successful exploitation of the environment. Changes in technology—culture—often resulted in anatomical changes. Tools that could cut, grind, and mash food took much of the burden off jaws and chewing muscles. With less work to do, jaws reduced in size. Because large teeth cannot fit in smaller jaws, natural selection favored smaller teeth as well.

Anatomical demands also had cultural consequences. Walking upright requires a compact pelvis to provide sufficient support. However, larger skull size (for larger brains) necessitates a wider birth canal. The balance struck by natural selection is the birth of children at a time when they can fit through the pelvic canal, but a time when they are immature and greatly dependent on their parents and community for their care. Thus, biological and anatomical aspects of evolution directly influence social life, with immature offspring needing years of nurturance, protection, and teaching.

Human health and illness provide another example of the interrelationship of biology and culture, both in modern times and in the past. Different methods of securing food and different types of social organization leave populations vulnerable to different sorts of illnesses. Small, mobile groups of hunter–gatherers don't often experience epidemics of infectious disease. Limited population size curbs high rates of infection, and moving from site to site limits problems caused by poor sanitation and contaminated water supplies. In agricultural societies, however, populations are larger and sedentary, allowing infectious diseases to take hold. Cultural practices such as the use of domesticated animals to help in the fields increase exposure to potentially contaminated waste products. Industrialization brings its own health risks and benefits.

In modern times, we see powerful ways in which cultural and social factors are brought to bear on biological well-being. Improved sanitation, immunization, insect control, and antibiotics are all cultural innovations that have had positive effects. However, poverty, pollution, discrimination, war, environmental change, and lack of access to health care have dire physiological consequences. Both biology and culture are factors in disease; likewise, disease has effects that are both biological and social. The current AIDS epidemic not only has sickened and killed millions but also has profoundly changed the fabric of society in a variety of ways. AIDS has engendered fear and discrimination, inspired scientific research and humanitarianism, restructured households and communities, and rewritten laws and literature.

### Cultural Anthropology Connects

Culture is a central concept of anthropology, and **cultural anthropologists** investigate the diversity of belief and behavior across societies. However, as we have seen, this subdiscipline is connected to and dependent on the other three.

Cultural rules differ from biological laws, but culture has the power to shape human biology. Conrad Kottak (2002) describes the ways in which culture acts as an environmental force to sculpt the human form. Culture differentially encourages some activities and abilities and discourages others. For example, particular sports result in very distinctive physical development. Cultural standards of beauty often mitigate against participation. Kottak suggests that Brazilian women avoid competitive swimming largely because it produces a bulky, muscular body type that runs counter to the ideal of Brazilian female beauty, which is softer and more curvaceous.

The choice of mates is another way in which culture influences biology. Learned preferences and cultural rules influence gene frequencies when individuals select or avoid particular partners, mating with individuals of the same height or with different hair color.

A classic example of the interaction between culture and biology is that of the sickle cell gene. Sickle cell anemia, a condition in which the red blood cells are misshapen and unable to deliver oxygen efficiently, is a potentially fatal disease. Healthy individuals possess two alleles for normal hemoglobin, the oxygen transport protein in red blood cells. Those with sickle cell anemia have two alleles for the abnormal hemoglobin. Scientists were surprised to find populations in Africa, India, and the Mediterranean with high frequencies of one abnormal hemoglobin allele until it was determined that although having two alleles for sickled cells was disastrous, having only one acted as protection against malaria. The geographic distribution of the sickle cell trait is very close to that of malaria. In malarial environments, it is advantageous to have one abnormal allele rather than two normal ones. In the early 1970s, biological anthropologist Frank Livingstone, seeking to explain the distribution of the sickle cell trait, demonstrated the ways in which culture played a role in shaping this genetic picture. Thousands of years ago, the dense forests of Africa did not harbor the mosquito that carries malaria, which thrives in sunlight and pools of stagnant water. However, the introduction of horticulture brought great ecological change and fertile breeding grounds to mosquitoes. Land was cleared to plant crops, allowing sunlight to reach the earth. Changes in the soil resulted in standing pools of water conducive to the growth of malaria-carrying mosquitoes. Settled villages grew larger in this abundant new economy, providing the population density that allowed the disease to spread. Thus, we see a connection between culture and biology: cultural adaptations (tools to clear land and horticulture) altered the ecology of the land and allowed malaria-carrying mosquitoes to greatly increase in number, which in turn led ultimately to the increased frequency of the sickle cell allele in the settled population (Relethford 2000). This example also underscores the importance of the holistic perspective in the work of individual anthropologists. As Erika Bourguignon (1996) points out, although Livingstone was attempting to answer a biological question, it was necessary for him to investigate and understand data from all four fields of anthropology. The distribution of language groups shed light on migration patterns. Archaeology provided evidence of iron tools used to clear the land. The shift from mobile hunting and gathering to settled agricultural villages yielded an entirely different social structure. Thus, it took all four subdisciplines of anthropology to understand the complexity of sickle cell anemia, its distribution, and why it still exists in many parts of the world.

### Anthropology Connects

Anthropologist Marvin Harris has pointed out that anthropologists don't view holism as an end in and of itself; rather, they have embraced the holistic perspective because it is "crucial for solving major riddles of human existence" (1997:25). James Peacock (1988) recounts a tale that exemplifies the pitfalls of looking too closely at the parts and not the whole: a factory worker, at the end of each day, would leave the gate pushing a wheelbarrow. Each day, the guard at the gate would stop the worker, check to make sure the wheelbarrow was empty, and only then allow the worker to exit. Not until several months later was it discovered that the worker had been stealing wheelbarrows. Anthropology's investigation into the wonders of the origins and diverse workings of human life is ongoing, our endeavors in each subdiscipline connected to the other three, always aiming to avoid the factory guard's error of inspecting the contents without regard to the container.

# REFERENCES

BERNARD, H. R.
  1980. Personal communication to Patricia Rice.
BONVILLAIN, N.
  1997. *Language, Culture, and Communication: The Meaning of Messages.* Upper Saddle River, NJ: Prentice Hall.
BOURGUIGNON, E.
  1996. "American Anthropology: A Personal View." *General Anthropology* 3(1):1–7.
ECKHOLM, E.
  2002. "Desire for Sons Drives Use of Prenatal Scans in China." *The New York Times,* June 21.
EHRENREICH, R.
  1996. "Archaeology: Integrating the Sciences and the Humanities." *Anthropology Newsletter,* March 16.
HARRIS, M.
  1997. "Anthropology Needs Holism; Holism Needs Anthropology." In *The Teaching of Anthropology: Problems, Issues, and Decisions,* edited by Conrad Phillip Kottak, Jane J. White, Richard H. Furlow, and Patricia C. Rice, pp. 22–28. Mountain View, CA: Mayfield Publishing Company.
HICKERSON, N. P.
  1997. "How to Save Linguistic Anthropology." In *The Teaching of Anthropology: Problems, Issues, and Decisions,* edited by Conrad Phillip Kottak, Jane J. White, Richard H. Furlow, and Patricia C. Rice, pp. 154–64. Mountain View, CA: Mayfield Publishing Company.
JOLLY, C. J. and R. WHITE
  1995. *Physical Anthropology and Archaeology.* New York: McGraw-Hill.
KOTTAK, C. P.
  2002. *Anthropology: The Exploration of Human Diversity.* New York: McGraw-Hill.
NANDA, S. and R. WARMS
  1998. *Cultural Anthropology.* Belmont, CA: Wadsworth.
PEACOCK, J. L.
  1988. *The Anthropological Lens: Harsh Light, Soft Focus.* Cambridge, UK: Cambridge University Press.
RELETHFORD, J. H.
  2000. *The Human Species: An Introduction to Biological Anthropology* (5th edition). New York: McGraw-Hill.
SAPIR, E.
  1997. (1912) In Bonvillain, N., *Language, Culture, and Communications: The Meaning of Messages.* Upper Saddle River, NJ: Prentice Hall.
SCHULTZ, E. A. and R. H. LAVENDA
  1998. *Anthropology: A Perspective on the Human Condition* (2nd edition). Mountain View, CA: Mayfield Publishing Company.
SCUPIN, R. and C. R. DECORSE
  2001. *Anthropology: A Global Perspective.* Upper Saddle River, NJ: Prentice Hall.
WILLCOX, D.
  1986. *Hmong Folklife.* Marion, North Carolina: Copple House Books.

# Thinking Theoretically

PHILIP CARL SALZMAN, McGill University

What do anthropologists mean when they talk about theories such as cultural materialism, structuralism, or postmodernism (Salzman 2001)? How do these theories relate to what anthropologists study? How exactly do anthropologists, and how exactly can you, think theoretically? And why do they, and why would you, want to think theoretically?

## THE PARTICULAR AND THE GENERAL

Anthropologists in their ethnographic field research on particular cultures look for patterns of thought, belief, activity, organization, and behavior. (See Chapter 2.) When patterns are identified they are sometimes called customs, norms, institutions, worldviews, or structures. Particular patterns can be identified with a specific time and place, such as the Trobriand Islands in the second decade of the twentieth century, Nuerland in the 1930s, Tikopia in the 1930s, Baluchistan in the 1960s and 1970s, or highland Sardinia in the 1990s. A. R. Radcliffe-Brown (1952:1), an originator of British social anthropology, called patterns found in a particular place and time **idiographic** because they are unique and specific to those times and places. Another term that could be used for these specific patterns is **descriptive**. By this we mean that the pattern discussed is close to the facts at a low **level of abstraction** from the particulars of a time and place.

But anthropologists are also interested in theory, which is general rather than particular, at a high rather than low level of abstraction. Theory is far from the facts of a specific time and place because it is intended to encompass a wide range of various specifics. Radcliffe-Brown (1952:1) called the quest for general knowledge **nomothetic** (meaning "law giving"), to distinguish it from the search for idiographic facts. Most anthropologists today would just call general formulations **theory.** The main point is that facts tied to particular times and places are specific, whereas theory is general and encompasses many facts from many times and places.

## HEURISTIC THEORIES

The most general theories I call **heuristic** theories, which means theories that guide our inquiries. Heuristic theories are very general in the sense that they are very abstract and purport to cover myriad facts from many times and places. Robert Merton (1957:9) describes such theories as "general orientations toward data, suggesting types of variables [factors that can vary, such as type of religion or marriage practices] that need somehow to be taken into account, rather than clear, verifiable statements of relationships between specified variables."

The dominant heuristic theory in the first half of the twentieth century was **functionalism.** In the functionalist perspective, society was understood as having a number of distinct parts, such as the institutions of politics, religion, and economics, that were interconnected with one another and mutually influential. In the functionalist perspective, any particular custom, rule, activity, or practice could be understood in relation to the other parts of the society in terms of its function for the other parts and the whole of society. For example, ancestor cults, praying to and leaving offerings for dead ancestors, were seen as an ideological support and rationale for lineage group organization in which all group members are descended from common ancestors (Colson 1962: Chapter 1). In this case, the "distinct parts" that influence each other are religion (ancestor cults) and social organization (lineages). Another related example is the functionalist argument that kinship terminologies and norms for relationships between kin, such as whether the relationships are strict and authoritative or warm and supportive, reflect group organization, with relations between seniors and juniors in the same descent group being strict and authoritative and those in different descent groups being warm and supportive (Radcliffe-Brown 1952: Chapter 2).

Thus functionalism offered a vision of the world and how it works and so directed anthropologists to focus their research on the elements and relations identified by the theory. Anthropologists under the influence of functionalism were guided in their ethnographic field research to search for functional interconnections between customs, practices, and institutions. In their analyses functionalist anthropologists explained customs, rules, and activities by their functions, by the effects of specific practices, beliefs, and norms on other institutions and practices, or by their effects on the continuity and existence of the society as a whole.

Heuristic theories guide anthropological thought by offering a vision of social and cultural reality and directing attention to what it deems is important. Each heuristic theory proposes a way of looking at the world, a way of carrying out research, and a way of understanding research findings. Functionalism did that for the first half of the twentieth century, and many anthropologists continue to be influenced by functionalist heuristics in their research.

Let us examine a more recent heuristic theory. **Cultural materialism** (Harris 1979) draws on the broad stream of Marxist materialism but adds an anthropological flavor. The main principle of cultural materialism is called infrastructural determinism (Harris 1979:56) and is expressed this way:

> The etic behavioral modes of production and reproduction probabilistically determine the etic behavioral domestic and political economy, which in turn probabilistically determine the behavioral and mental emic structures. (Harris 1979:55–56)

This means that (1) the infrastructure, how people make a living and reproduce, shapes (2) the structure, how people organize themselves, and how they organize themselves shapes (3) the superstructure, people's ideas and such activities as ritual, art, and sports. Harris (1979:26–27) says explicitly that cultural materialism is a "research strategy"—in our terms, a heuristic theory—to guide research. But its goal is very ambitious:

> The aim of cultural materialism in particular is to account for the origin, maintenance, and change of the global inventory of socio-cultural differences and similarities. (Harris 1979:27)

In this sense, cultural materialism is a heuristic theory *par excellence*. It should explain everything!

How would cultural materialism guide an anthropologist's thoughts and research? First, the anthropologist would want to be sure to collect information on the infrastructure, structure, and superstructure in order to see the relations between them. Second, the anthropologist would want to know clearly what information or data collected is **etic,** based on observation on people's activities, and which information is **emic,** based on people's ideas. Third, the anthropologist would seek explanation for any particular custom, practice, or belief in the infrastructure, that is, technology of subsistence, technoenvironmental relations, work patterns, mating patterns, or demography.

An example of cultural materialism is Harris's (1966, 1974) examination of sacred cattle in India. Harris wants to know why "clean caste" Hindus of India believe that cows are sacred and that cows must not be killed and their meat must not be eaten. There are tens of millions of cattle in India, but they are not slaughtered, and their meat is forbidden to Hindus. Surely plenty of Indians could use the nourishment, so why do they abstain?

Harris's first answer is that Hindus abstain from eating beef because it is sacred. The cultural rule that forbids Hindus to eat beef is very important because it overrules immediate individual needs and thus serves the long-term needs of the collectivity. Harris's second answer is that Indian cattle are a critical contributor to the vegetarian diet of caste Hindus. Unlike beef, the milk and butter oil (ghee) that cattle contribute to the Indian diet are renewable. Cattle dung serves as fertilizer for the grain fields and for fuel. And cattle pull the plows for grain cultivation. Because the grain, milk, and vegetable diet of Hindus is very efficiently produced, it can support the large Indian population. In contrast, enough meat could be produced to support only a small percentage of the Indian population. In short, Indian cattle are thought to be sacred because they must be protected to make their contribution to the efficient Hindu vegetarian diet. Here Harris is arguing that the explanation for a religious belief is found in the way people make a living.

Heuristic theories such as functionalism and cultural materialism provide the anthropologist with a general approach to the world and to research and offer guidelines for thinking about and commenting on research findings. Because heuristic theories are so general, they cannot be disproved in themselves. There is no one finding that can show that a heuristic theory is wrong. If a functional relationship is not found, a functionalist critic could say that the researcher did not look hard enough. If in a cultural materialist analysis, infrastructural determination cannot be found, Harris would say that the determination is probabilistic and exists in most cases if not in this exception. So heuristic theories cannot really be tested to see whether they are true or false but instead are generally judged to be useful or not useful, fruitful or not fruitful in generating interesting results.

## SUBSTANTIVE THEORIES

A second kind of theory we can call **substantive theories** in that they specify a definite relationship between two or more sets or categories of social and cultural phenomena. They are more specific and particular than heuristic theories, but they are more general than descriptions tied to particular times and places. Robert Merton (1957:9) called these theories **middle-range theories** because they are less abstract than grand or heuristic theory but more abstract than descriptions of particular cases. Thus it is easier to bring data or evidence to bear on these theories to test whether they hold up in the face of descriptive, ethnographic case material. Substantive or middle-range theories therefore can be judged in a more definitive fashion as to whether they are correct.

As an example, let us examine Julian Steward's (1963: Chapter 7) theory of the patrilineal band. Steward was studying hunters and gatherers. He found that some are patrilineal and patrilocal, that is, as a group they are constituted as descendants of a common ancestor in the male line, and when the men marry they stay at home, but women who marry outside the group go to live with their husbands. The patrilineal hunting band differs from other hunters who lived as independent families or whose bands were composite, with no unity based on common descent, and with men and women coming from other groups and going to other groups. Steward asked what explains the presence of the patrilineal hunting band rather than separate families or composite bands.

Drawing on his knowledge of many different hunting groups, Steward formulated a theory that specified exactly the conditions in which patrilineal bands would be found. He argues, having cited case material from the Bushmen of southern Africa, central African Negritos, Semang from Malaya, Philippine Negritos, and Australian Aborigines, that four factors produce the patrilineal band (1963:135):

1. A population density of one person or less—usually much less—per square mile, which is caused by a hunting and gathering technology in areas of scarce wild foods;

2. An environment in which the principal food is game that is nonmigratory and scattered, which makes it advantageous for men to remain in the general territory of their birth;

3. Transportation restricted to human carriers;

4. The cultural-psychological fact, which cannot be explained by local adaptation, that groups of kin who associate together intimately tend to extend incest taboos from the biological family to the extended family, thus requiring group exogamy.

Note that although the relationship between the form to be explained, the patrilineal band, and the four conditions underlying it is specified in a definite fashion, the theory is somewhat abstract, dealing with categories of phenomena—patrilineal bands and four conditions—rather than one unique case limited in space and time. The definiteness of the relationship specified allows us to test the theory. By looking at some other cases of hunting groups, such as the Inuit (Eskimo) of arctic America or the Kwakiutl of the northwest coast of North America, we can check to see whether the relationship specified by Steward holds up. If we were to find a patrilineal hunting group that depended on migratory game rather than nonmigratory and scattered game (Steward's third condition) or a nonpatrilineal composite band that seems to fulfill Steward's four conditions, we would throw serious doubt on Steward's theory.

Substantive or middle-range theories can be inspired by heuristic theories. This is what Harris intended in formulating his cultural materialist research strategy:

> Cultural materialism shares with other scientific strategies an epistemology which seeks to restrict fields of inquiry to events, entities, and relationships that are knowable by means of explicit, logico-empirical, inductive-deductive, quantifiable public procedures or "operations" subject to replication by independent observers. (1979:27)

Harris's "explicit, logico-empirical, inductive-deductive, quantifiable public procedures" are the testing of substantive, middle-range theories.

Not all heuristic theories lead to or are consistent with explicit, substantive, middle-range theories. The reason for this is that not all heuristic theories are consistent with a scientific approach to studying society and culture. Science aims at explanation, the identification of causal relationships, which requires substantive or middle-range theories. In contrast, some anthropological heuristic theories are more oriented to the humanities and advocate explication rather than explanation. Explication usually involves exploring the meaning that ideas and actions, patterns and practices have for the people involved. Explication thus tends to focus on elaboration of the specific and particular rather than attempting to relate causal factors in middle-range theories.

The most influential humanistic heuristic theory is **interpretationalism,** invented almost singlehandedly by Clifford Geertz and first elucidated in *The Interpretation of Cultures* (1973). His focus is on meaning:

> The concept of culture I espouse . . . is essentially a semiotic one. Believing, with Max Weber, that man is an animal suspended in webs of significance he himself has spun, I take culture to be those webs, and the analysis of it to be therefore not an experimental science in search of law but an interpretive one in search of meaning. It is explication I am after, construing social expressions on their surface enigmatical. (1973:5)

By saying that he is not in search of "law," Geertz is saying that he is not trying to find scientific laws or substantive theories to explain human life. Geertz elaborates:

> As interworked systems of construable signs (. . . symbols), culture is not a power, something to which social events, behaviors, institutions, or processes can be causally attributed; it is a context, something within which they can be intelligibly–that is, thickly–described. (1973:14)

Geertz's alternative to substantive, middle-range theory is "thick description," an elaborate account of the many meanings involved in any specific human activity in any particular time and place. So, for Geertz, there is heuristic theory as a guide and thick description, with no substantive theory in between.

Partly under the influence of Geertz and interpretive anthropology, a more recent heuristic theory, **postmodernism** (Marcus and Fischer 1986; Clifford and Marcus 1986; Marcus 1998), rejects a scientific approach and all empiricism and positivism in anthropology as false and politically suspect, and rejects any "master narrative" as one sided. Postmodernism stresses the subjectivity of the researcher and the injustice in treating the subjects of research, the people being studied, as objects. Rejecting any formulation of scientific, substantive, middle range theories, postmodernism has stressed giving "voice" to the subjects of research so that they can tell their own stories rather than have our theories or interpretations imposed on them. So postmodernism too goes directly from heuristic theory to "voice," with no intermediate theoretical formulation.

## THEORIES IN PALEOANTHROPOLOGY

Archaeologists, who study people's culture in the past, are closer to cultural anthropologists in terms of their use of theories than biological anthropologists because they share culture as their central focus, and it is theories that help us explain culture, thus tying the two anthropological subfields. Additionally, American archaeologists, brought up in the New World intellectual tradition that claims "archaeology is anthropology," would make only one change in this essay to be compatible with their own concepts of theory: they would put everything in the past tense because they focus on people's culture in the past. They would agree there are heuristic theories and many still ascribe to functionalism to see how cultures in the past worked. Others are materialists, to some extent because the nature of their data is material culture and they often "force" material items to tell stories even larger than the items themselves. But they would add a third heuristic theory, called ecoculturalism, which is also a guide to archaeological inquiries because within the long time frame archaeologists work with, climate changes. All anthropologists, but particularly ecoculturalists, firmly believe cultures exist in an environmental context and if the climate changes, so will the culture. Ecoculturalism therefore is often used by archaeologists as a causal explanation for change. By contrast, cultural anthropologists do not normally study groups long enough to use environmental change as causal.

Particularly since 1960, archaeologists under the banner of Lewis Binford (1972, 1977) have embraced middle-range theory to attempt to explain why cultures were the way they were in the past. They focus on experiments and analysis of topics not tied to a particular time or place to see whether their assumptions are supported. For example, in the 1950s Russian archaeologist Sergei Semenov (1964), working alone in St. Petersburg, discovered the principles of microwear analysis in an attempt to explain the function of prehistoric flint tools. He used artifacts in the collections at St. Petersburg that were obviously mostly from prehistoric Russian times. Would these principles be applicable to microwear on tools in prehistoric France or prehistoric Africa? Middle-range theory tested this idea through comparisons of collections and through "blind tests" in which one experimenter made and used a number of different kinds of tools, leaving different kinds of microwear on them, and the second experimenter looked at the tools (after they had been washed to make sure no clues were left behind) and their microwear and came to conclusions as to their function (Keeley and Newcomer 1977). Postmodernism has its advocates in archaeology as well, but although postmodern archaeologists criticize other theoretical positions and reject all scientific procedures and logical positivism (see Chapter 7), they have not produced work that has advanced our understanding of the past.

Biological anthropologists, by contrast, listen to a different theoretical drummer. With few exceptions, biological anthropologists are Darwinian scientists. That means that as they attempt to understand human evolution and the state of modern humans today, they do so under the strict guidance of Darwinian principles. They ask, How did natural selection favor bipedalism? Why were brains late in becoming larger? Why do people who live around the equator today have darker skins than those who live further away? One of Darwin's tenets in evolution was that regardless of cause (most of which he did not understand in 1850), because of millions of years of evolution, populations were at any time well adapted to their environments. So to what was bipedalism adapted? Why did change from four-leggedness to two-leggedness better adapt hominids (prehumans) to their environment?

Although biological anthropologists study humans just as archaeologists and cultural anthropologists do, one of the big differences between them is in their explanatory theories. Biological anthropologists adhere to one theory, natural selection, which, if Darwin was correct, yields adaptation. By contrast, cultural anthropologists choose from among several kinds of theories to guide them in finding explanations. Nonetheless, all anthropologists, no matter what their specialization, think theoretically because it guides what they see and how they interpret what they see to explain the human condition.

## HOW CAN YOU THINK THEORETICALLY?

Whenever we think about things or look at things, we are guided by a heuristic theory. That theory may be an implicit one based on "American culture" and be considered "common sense," or it may be an explicit one based on our religion or our political position, or it may be an explicit one based in an academic discipline such as anthropology, economics, history, or literary criticism. What we assume is important, what we look for, what we expect to find, and the very categories and their labels are based in our heuristic theories. (See Chapter 7 for a discussion of biases, assumptions, and preconceptions in research.)

One important step in thinking theoretically is being aware of our heuristics, making explicit our guiding theory, and giving attention to its assumptions and implications. In other words, part of thinking theoretically is bringing heuristic theory into our consciousness and taking a critical stance to it. By being aware of our own heuristic theories, we are able to proceed in a more self-critical and intellectually more responsible fashion.

Another step in thinking theoretically is being aware that any account, anthropological or other, of society or culture is based on heuristic theory, whether or not that is made explicit. Let's say we are reading a book on mortuary ritual in Melanesia that seems pretty descriptive (maybe too descriptive for our taste). But even if the author is not explicit about the heuristic approach, the author's treatment of mortuary ritual will reflect the author's heuristic theory. So we have to ask ourselves, "What is the guiding heuristic theory?" For example, if the author is a cultural materialist, there will be an attempt to explain mortuary ritual (which would be regarded as superstructure) in terms of forms of social organization (structure) or the way people make a living (infrastructure). But if the author is an interpretive anthropologist, mortuary ritual would be explicated in terms of the wider realms of meaning, such as the people's metaphysics (for example, their ideas about the continuing influence of dead ancestors or about an afterlife or rebirth), theology (for example, ideas about gods or God, about final judgment), and social assumptions (for example, whether social rank continues after death). Thinking theoretically means knowing the theoretical background of the various accounts and reports and commentaries offered by anthropologists or anyone else.

The third step in thinking theoretically is explicitly relating your own work, in writing papers or writing exams, to your theoretical assumptions and framework and to the theoretical frameworks, both heuristic and substantive, important in anthropology or other relevant fields. In other words, however much you are focused on reporting facts, you must relate these to the theories of the authors and to the other theories prevalent in anthropology. So it is necessary to be familiar with the theories and to be able to see when they underlay or influence the discussion and to be able to explain this as part of your own presentations.

Finally, thinking theoretically means working with theory, whether heuristic or substantive, in your own thinking and presentations. Other people's theoretical formulations, even those of illustrious anthropologists, are not the final word, but can be used as bases on which to develop and elaborate theoretical ideas. Let me give a simple example from my own thinking when I was a student. Merton (1957) spoke about manifest and latent functions of customs and institutions: manifest functions were desired and recognized consequences, whereas latent functions were undesired and unrecognized consequences. If sexual freedom was a manifest function of the sexual revolution of the 1960s, children being born to single, teenage mothers is a latent function of the sexual revolution. But it occurred to me that some consequences could also be desired but unrecognized, such as (this may or may not be true) children's increased intellectual power resulting from watching television, or could be undesired but recognized, such as sending kids to school reducing parental authority and control. Although this little conceptual innovation was no great sociological breakthrough, and I gained no great fame from it, my teachers were a little bit impressed. Most important, it helped me along the road to thinking theoretically.

## REFERENCES

BINFORD, L. R.
    1972. *An Archaeological Perspective*. New York: Seminar Press.
    1977. *For Theory Building in Archaeology*. Orlando, FL: Academic Press.
CLIFFORD, J. and G. E. MARCUS, eds.
    1986. *Writing Culture: The Poetics and Politics of Ethnography*. Berkeley: University of California Press.
COLSON, E.
    1962. *The Plateau Tonga of Northern Rhodesia*. Manchester: Manchester University Press.

GEERTZ, C.
    1973. *The Interpretation of Cultures.* New York: Basic Books.
HARRIS, M.
    1966. "The Cultural Ecology of Indian's Sacred Cattle." *Current Anthropology* 7:51–66.
    1974. *Cows, Pigs, Wars and Witches: The Riddles of Culture.* New York: Random House.
    1979. *Cultural Materialism.* New York: Random House.
KEELEY, L. and M. NEWCOMER
    1977. "Microwear Analysis of Experimental Flint Tools: A Test Case." *Journal of Archaeological Science* 4:29–62.
MARCUS, G. E.
    1998. *Ethnography through Thick and Thin.* Princeton, NJ: Princeton University Press.
MARCUS, G. E. and M. J. FISCHER, eds.
    1986. *Anthropology and Cultural Critique: An Experimental Moment in the Human Sciences.* Chicago: University of Chicago Press.
MERTON, R.
    1957. *Social Theory and Social Structure.* Glencoe, IL: Free Press.
RADCLIFFE-BROWN, A. R.
    1952. *Structure and Function in Primitive Society.* London: Cohen and West.
SALZMAN, P. C.
    2001. *Understanding Culture: An Introduction to Anthropological Theory.* Prospect Heights, IL: Waveland.
SEMENOV, S. A.
    1964. *Prehistoric Technology.* New York: Barnes & Noble.
STEWARD, J.
    1963. *Theory of Culture Change.* Urbana: University of Illinois Press.

# Using Science to Think Anthropologically[1]

ROBIN O'BRIAN, *Elmira College*
PATRICIA C. RICE, *West Virginia University*

Geoff Clark, a well-known expert on the Spanish Upper Paleolithic period, said to one of us recently, "I am a scientist first, an anthropologist second, and an archaeologist third." By using this order, he is stating that he thinks like a scientist first (method), like an anthropologist second (broad-based content), and like an archaeologist last (specific content). No matter what our specialization in anthropology, we must first and foremost think scientifically, and as a student of anthropology, you must think scientifically too. How do we do this?

Science is a way of thinking about something. It is a method of inquiry. It does not necessarily involve bubbling retorts or white lab coats. Because scientists believe there is an orderly world out there where events (past or present) can be explained if adequate observation or data are used properly, that world can be known. And it is **knowledge** that scientists are searching for. Science goes beyond data gathering and description to explain things and happenings.

For example, **biological anthropologists** do not just excavate and then describe fossils of our ancestors who lived before us; they attempt to explain why there has been change between then and now and, if there is a large enough sample, why one fossil looks different from one that is the same age. **Archaeologists** don't just describe the flint tools they excavate; they try to explain how those tools were used. And although it seems quite different, other anthropologists use what people do and say as the data they examine. A **cultural anthropologist** doing research in rural India might note that there is a widespread presence of cattle even in areas of malnutrition and wonder why people do not eat beef (Harris 1965). A specialist in **linguistics** in the same neighborhood would note the symbols for sounds in the language spoken by the people and then attempt to figure out how they can engage in trade with a neighboring group who speak a totally different language.

Scientists do not have to use statistics or do experiments to do science. All they have to do is to think scientifically. To think scientifically is to do science, and doing science concerns its method. What scientists use is **the scientific method**. The scientific method begins with something worth investigating, some question for which we do not have an answer. If there is a question, there is probably more than one possible answer to it. When the question is stated with a possible answer, it becomes a **hypothesis**. Put another way, a hypothesis is a good guess about something. Here are some anthropological examples. "I hypothesize that modern humans were on Earth about 100,000 years ago." This is a good guess based on existing fossil finds and modern dating techniques. "He hypothesized that many more tools could be made from a flint nodule if the flint knapper made blades instead of flakes." This is a good guess based on previous flint knapping experiments by a flint knapper. (Note: Flint knapping is making modern tools of flint using techniques deduced from observing marks on prehistoric tools.) "I hypothesize that Indian farmers don't eat their cattle because they are more useful as plow animals, and if they eat them they won't be able to farm." This is a good guess based on observation and talking with the farmers. Finally, "I hypothesize that the group in question can trade with neighbors who do not speak their language because what they are trading is very valuable to them, and they are able to do the actual trade through gestures." This is also a good guess based again on observation (the gestures) and talking to the people involved.

Whichever hypothesis you want to follow through on, the fossil, the artifact, the customs, or the language, the next step is to attempt to discover whether it is false or supported. Many interesting things cannot be falsified and therefore are not subject to scientific investigation. Some of us would like to know whether the Tooth Fairy exists, but hypothesizing that it does exist (or does not) is not scientific because the hypothesis cannot be falsified.

To **test** any of these hypotheses, the scientist-anthropologist would have to gather data pertinent to the question asked to falsify or support it. You can't gather and use data on penguins to answer a question about human burial rituals. The fossils, artifacts, observations on customs, and tape recordings of the spoken language are all considered **evidence** or **data** and are used to support or falsify a particular hypothesis. If the evidence supports the hypothesis, it is supported; if not, it is falsified.

Testing hypotheses is not the solitary job of a single scientist testing and retesting his or her own work. Other scientists take a skeptical position and retest the hypothesis to see whether they get the same results. If the same data and methods are used, **replication** can support or refute the hypothesis. Thus, science is a collective rather than an individual enterprise.

Hypotheses can be found to be false, but they cannot be proved because all of the data pertinent to answering the question are never available. We do not have the remains of all of the people who were alive 100,000 years ago, we do not have all of the flint blades and flakes ever made, we were not in India or New Guinea when most social customs originated, and we cannot watch every trading expedition. Scientists never use the terms "proof" or "prove" because they imply certainty. (Terms such as "scientific proof" are abominations, and the "P words" are common practice only in courtrooms.) The same is true of the word "truth" because it implies certainty beyond a shadow of a doubt. Scientists know better than to even claim they search for truth because it is unattainable. They are content with finding **knowledge,** defined as a description of something that is probably correct, given the available data. But if truth and proof are finite and non-changing, knowledge is changeable and fluid. Today's knowledge is yesterday's antiquated myth, and tomorrow's knowledge will show that half of what we think we know now is wrong. Scientists look for change in knowledge, and it is healthy to be skeptical about one's own work as well as that of others.

Some change in knowledge is slow in coming; some is very fast. As an example of slow change in knowledge, consider the transmission of biological traits from one generation to another. For thousands of years, people have certainly noticed that children look more like their parents than they look like strangers. Until the nineteenth century, scientists thought traits were carried in the blood; then Gregor Mendel devised his Laws of Inheritance, with 34 years elapsing until his ideas became known and accepted. Finally, it was another 50 years before we could speak of the beginning of modern genetics in the 1950s.

Other changes in knowledge are remarkably speedy, such as the discovery of the Ice Man, a mummy found on the Austrian–Italian border in the Alps in 1991. When first discovered, it was thought to be a casualty of the previous year's bad storm, but the condition of the body tissue suggested it was old. At first, it was dated as perhaps 2,000 years old, but more recently, carbon 14 dating dated the mummy at 5,300 years ago. As to the cause of his death, early knowledge suggested that he froze to death, and then the ice and snow desiccated his tissue, mummifying it. Very recently, a computed axial tomography (CAT) scan discovered an arrow in his shoulder, and it is now believed that this caused his death, directly or indirectly (Bahn 2002; Fowler 2000). At any point in the past decade, our knowledge about the Ice Man was based on the data we had at that time, but as additional evidence became available, our knowledge changed. And it will continue to change. It is a good thing that none of the scientists involved claimed to have "proved" anything!

There are two variations of the scientific method in terms of the order of steps taken to go from interesting findings to conclusions. If a hypothesis is generated about something interesting before any data are gathered (observations made, people talked to, languages heard), the type of science is called **deductive science.** That hypothesis could have come from someone else's previous work that the particular scientist did not agree with, or it could have come from a brainstorming session with other scientists over a beer at the end of a day, or it could have come in a dream. The point is that it is a good guess about something, as in "I bet they can trade with their neighbors through gesture even if they can't understand each other." In deductive science, the scientist then gathers appropriate data to see whether it supports that guess. If it does, it is supported; if not, it was a bad guess. The other variation is called **inductive science.** In inductive methods, data about a particular subject of interest are freely gathered, with no preconceived idea of whether they will answer any question or how they would answer any question. Out of the data gathering and analysis comes a conclusion about that subject, and that conclusion becomes the hypothesis. Now different data must be gathered to test the hypothesis for support or falsification. So, regardless of where in the process one begins, the process is the same: hypothesis, data gathering, data analysis, conclusions.

Here are some examples of inductively and deductively generated research projects:

Everyone "knows" that 25,000-year-old Venus statuettes from the European Upper Paleolithic period and carved from ivory, bone, or precious stone were fertility dolls. Right? Not necessarily. A female anthropologist wondered whether the anthropologists who had studied Venus statuettes previously—all male—were biased by the obvious nakedness of the statuettes and attributed fertility to them because of it. She decided to look at every one of the 180 Venuses and assess each relative to its age (did the artist attempt to sculpt a young, middle-aged, or old woman?) and state of pregnancy (did the artist attempt to sculpt a pregnant woman?). After categorizing every possible Venus, the result was that only 17 percent of the statuettes were both in the right age category and obviously pregnant. Not only did this suggest that the fertility doll idea was incorrect, but the conclusions also led to a new hypothesis: women were sculpted because they provided most of the food eaten by the group, did become pregnant and have babies, and were the important focus of house and home (Rice 1981). New evidence was then gathered to support (or not) the new hypothesis. You should recognize this as **inductive** research because data were freely gathered, resulting in a hypothesis. It also suggests that male and female scientists observe the same things—in this case Venus statuettes—differently just because they are of different sexes. (See Chapter 7 for more examples of why scientists disagree.)

A specialist in prehistoric art published research that concluded that a painting on the ceiling of the famous 18,000-year-old Altamira ceiling was a bison, not a wild boar, as previous experts believed. Another specialist in prehistoric art in turn questioned the bison identification of the animal and set out to find data to support the hypothesis that it was a boar after all. This specialist measured various points on the animal in question, other bison and boars in cave art, and live bison and boars and came up with four ratios that described the shape of the two animals (relative leg length and body shape). By comparing the ratios of all of the animals, the specialist found that the animal in question matched the boar, not the bison (Rice 1992). You should recognize this as **deductive** research because the researcher had already generated the hypothesis ("It is a boar") before collecting any data (the ratios).

If you wonder whether Maya women become farmers because there is increasing economic need where they live and decide to test this hypothesis by conducting research in southern Mexico, this is deductive science because your hypothesis, "Rural Maya women will enter farming because of economic need," precedes your trip to Mexico. You have already predicted a reason for the Maya women to become farmers. But when you arrive and discover that indeed there is economic need but that women are becoming commercial weavers, not farmers, your hypothesis is disproved. So, like any good researcher, you collect a lot of data about women weavers. You ask them about where they live, what they weave, and how they learned to weave, and about their friends, communities, religions, and families. This is inductive science because the data were gathered freely, with no assumed question asked. Although this sounds a good deal like plain conversation, and it is, it is also more evidence for other questions you might ask. When you return from your field work and analyze your evidence, if you discover that Maya women who live in urban settings and are Protestant converts don't know how to weave and sell commercially made crafts, whereas rural women who still learn weaving from their mothers sell traditional hand-woven crafts, this becomes an inductive hypothesis ("Protestant women are less likely than Catholic women to know and use traditional weaving skills") that arose after you collected your data (O'Brian 1994). You would probably return to collect new data, perhaps quantitative, to support or reject that hypothesis and then perhaps move into some of the "why" questions. Research generates further research.

The word **hypothesis** has another scientific meaning related to the **level of confidence** a scientist has about the results of an investigation. If a scientist has a medium amount of confidence in a conclusion, perhaps because he or she did the actual work, the phrase "the hypothesis is supported" is appropriate. If that hypothesis is tested and retested by many different scientists over a period of years and it is still supported (not rejected or found to be false), its level of confidence raises it to the level of a **theory.** When a theory has been around for a hundred years or more and hundreds of scientists have tried to disprove it with no luck, its level of confidence is extremely high, and we call it a **law.** Any one of these— hypothesis, theory, or law—can still be found to be false, but the higher the confidence level, the less likely it is to be found false. (See Chapter 4 for other meanings of "theory.")

For example, when Charles Darwin came up with the idea of natural selection, it was a hypothesis. It explained some observable things in nature, such as the shape of tortoise shells in the Gálapagos Islands, but there was a lot about nature that was still unknown, such as genetics. By the turn of the twentieth century, scientists knew about mutations and some genetic principles, and more of the biological world could be explained by natural selection. At this point, natural selection became a theory because the original hypothesis had gained in its level of confidence. It has now been close to 150 years since the *Origin of Species* was published, with thousands of scientists attempting to disprove natural selection. It has been tweaked and changed in places, but in general Darwin's version of natural selection has not changed. Our level of confidence in it gives it law-like status. Thus hypothesis, theory, law are places on a continuum of scientific confidence. Not much knowledge is law-like, the term "theory" tends to be overused, and thus most of what knowledge we have is in the form of hypotheses, ready to move to a higher level of confidence, if merited, or tested yet again to see whether it remains supported.

An example of a hypothesis in the bioarchaeological world of anthropology that is still being tested and retested concerns the role of Neandertal in modern human ancestry. The hypotheses could be stated either way. They were in our ancestry or they were not, and the hypothesis might be, "Neandertals were a separate species from *Homo sapiens* in Europe even though they overlapped there for more than 10,000 years." Some experts have tested the hypothesis by comparing fossils of the two populations, concluding that they differ in enough traits to call them different species and that they were not in our ancestry at all; some have retested it using mitochondrial DNA, concluding that there are too many differences for them to be a single species. These tests supported the hypotheses. But other experts point to a number of biological traits occurring more often in Neandertal than in the subsequent modern human invaders and claim that those traits have come about through interbreeding of the two populations. This rejects the hypothesis. (See Chapter 7 for further insights into this problem.) The point here is that scientists keep testing and retesting hypotheses, and in some cases new research supports and in some cases it rejects that hypothesis. Sometimes rejection removes the hypothesis from further study, whereas in the case of the Neandertal hypotheses, sides are so entrenched that the testing on both sides will continue.

A cultural example of testing and retesting refers to how people rear and understand children and teenagers, something that is of fundamental interest to most people. In the 1920s, Margaret Mead hypothesized that raising children in the traditional Polynesian society of Samoa would produce relaxed, easygoing teenagers. She suggested that they differed dramatically from American teenagers, who seemed full of emotional turmoil. Mead concluded that the seeming difference between Samoan and American teenagers meant that adolescence was strongly shaped by culture, not biology (Mead 1928).

Much later, in the 1980s, another anthropologist, Derek Freeman, using data he had collected from elsewhere in Samoa in the 1940s, argued that Samoan teenagers had a good deal of anxiety and turmoil, although they expressed it differently from Americans. He argued that, contrary to Mead, adolescence probably was a biological state experienced by teenagers in all cultures (Freeman 1983).

Freeman's work has been criticized by other anthropologists wanting to test his hypothesis. It appears that Mead and Freeman both were a little bit right and a little bit wrong and that at least some adolescent moodiness is biologically driven but that culture, the rules and ideas of a given society, shapes the way teenagers behave and express their emotions. The issue is not closed, and other cultural anthropologists will continue to test the biological and cultural hypotheses with data from groups they have studied.

What do scientists mean when they speak or write of **data** or **evidence?** How do they get it? What do they do with it? Anthropological data or evidence varies by subdiscipline. To a biological anthropologist, the data may come from excavating fossils, analyzing fossils found by others, or work on modern people. Some biological anthropologists, such as Meave Leakey, Alan Walker, Don Johanson, or Chris Beard, purposely look for fossils in our human lineage, Meave Leakey and Alan Walker at sites in Kenya looking for fossils that are in the neighborhood of 3 to 1 million years ago, Don Johanson in Ethiopia looking for fossils several million years older than this, and Chris Beard in China looking for the ancestors of the earliest primates some 40 million years ago. Other biological anthropologists compare single anatomical features through time, such as evidence of bipedalism or brain capacities.

Archaeologists normally use physical **artifacts** as their data or evidence. Artifacts often are tools: it has been estimated that 99 percent of all artifacts that have been collected are tools. Although tools are important because they tell archaeologists what people did for a living, often the nature of trade, and sometimes even social organization, the other 1 percent tells us even more: a bit of twine embossed in a chunk of clay tells us that 24,000 years ago, people were making twine and probably weaving cloth or making nets for fishing. Grains stuck in fired pottery can tell us what crops might have been domesticated. Cave paintings going back as early as 32,000 years ago and Venus figurines may tell us about social organization and the relative rank of the sexes in Paleolithic times (Rice and Paterson 1988). Finally, the finding of burials, shrines, or statuary may give us a glimpse of people's religion in prehistoric times. By definition, an artifact is any remains of something made by a human in the past, such as a tool, a cave painting, or a burial. They normally don't "speak for themselves," and have to be interpreted, but they are evidence nonetheless.

Culturally, evidence includes the tools people use, but it can also be people's behavior, their conversations and ideas, and their traditions and customs. For example, if an ethnographer visits people in a lowland Amazonian village and writes down whatever he observes them doing when he arrives and does this many times over the course of a number of months, he can discover, statistically, how people spend their days. Although the people may tell the ethnographer one thing—that men work harder than women, for example—the data from all of those visits might show that women work more because when families sit around and talk after a meal, women also busy themselves with tasks while men and children do not. Indeed, Allen Johnson (1975), working among the Machiguenga in Peru, found exactly that and showed how his careful collection of time allocation data provided results that surprised even him.

In this cultural example, all the simple things that people do in their daily lives have been transformed into evidence, and understanding its larger meaning depends on how the anthropologist collects and analyzes it. You can also see that the collection and analysis of data can show that what people say may not be accurate, and that in itself might suggest further questions to ask. In the example, you might want to ask why women's work seems less hard or why people seem to ignore it. This question, based on the analysis of your previous work, would lead you to more research.

## CONCLUSION

Thinking scientifically will put you in the proper attitude for thinking anthropologically, which in turn will allow you to think human biology, archaeology, linguistics, or cultural anthropology. When you read about current evidence supporting a particular hypothesis, remember that it is not necessarily the last word. New evidence may be discovered that forces scientists to change their conclusions and perhaps ask new questions. That means that you should be skeptical and keep an open mind, realizing that there are different degrees of confidence given to each finding, and that science is self-correcting. Today's factoids may be tomorrow's corrected knowledge. And science continues, getting better and better at explaining that knowable world out there.

## NOTE

1. Anthropologists do not all take the same approach to try to understand the world: humanistic anthropologists focus on cultural meaning, critical anthropologists focus on social evaluation and policy, and scientific anthropologists use the scientific method to explain what it is to be human. This chapter focuses on the scientific approach.

## REFERENCES

BAHN, P.
    2002. "A Most Mysterious Death." *Archaeology,* March/April:54.
FOWLER, B.
    2000. *Ice Man.* New York: Random House.
FREEMAN, D.
    1983. *Margaret Mead and Samoa: The Making and Unmaking of an Anthropological Myth.* Cambridge, MA: Harvard University Press.
HARRIS, M.
    1965. "The Cultural Ecology of India's Sacred Cattle." *Current Anthropology* 7:51–66.

JOHNSON, A. W.
    1975. "Time Allocation in a Machiguenga Community." *Ethnology* 14:301–310.
MEAD, M.
    1928. *Coming of Age in Samoa: A Psychological Study of Primitive Youth for Western Civilization.* New York: Morrow.
O'BRIAN, R.
    1994. *The Peso and the Loom: The Political Economy of Maya Women's Work in Highland Chiapas, Mexico.* PhD dissertation, UCLA.
RICE, P. C.
    1981. "Prehistoric Venuses: Symbols of Motherhood or Womanhood?" *Journal of Anthropological Research* 37(4):402–414.
    1992. "The Boars from Altamira: Solving an Identity Problem." *Papers from the Institute of Archaeology, University College London* 3:23–29.
RICE, P. C. and A. L. PATERSON
    1988. "Anthropomorphs in Cave Art: An Empirical Assessment." *American Anthropologist* 90(3):664–674.

# Thinking about Change

## Biological Evolution, Culture Change, and the Importance of Scale

JEFFREY H. COHEN *and* JEFFREY A. KURLAND,

*Pennsylvania State University*

Do your parents hate your favorite music? Do they ask you to turn it down or turn it off? Do they tell you that everything you listen to sounds the same? As you lower the volume, do you think to yourself, "Can't they hear the difference?" Now, imagine that a pair of anthropologists from a faraway planet show up at your door and enter your home. They ask to listen to your music. You play a new recording by your favorite band. After a song or two, they sit down with your parents and enjoy a few bars of your mother's Beethoven and your father's Beatles.

> The anthropologists listen a little longer and comment, "What is it with humans? All of your music sounds the same!"
> You respond, "Can't you hear the difference?"
> Your parents exclaim, "Don't tell us you like that noise."

The alien anthropologists sense an opportunity for an intergalactic exchange of ideas. They give you a mission: explain to them why not all human music is the same and why the differences that you hear matter. They remind you that they are not interested in your tastes or the disagreements you have with your parents. They want to understand the place and meaning of music in human culture and society.

In response to the aliens, your mother wonders, "Is the gamelan concert we heard last week at the university the same as Handel's *Messiah?*" Your parents lecture the aliens on the history of Western music from Gregorian chants of the eighth century to atonal music of the late twentieth century.

After 15 minutes you wake up and interrupt your parents, "What about the nineteenth-century gospel roots of rap and the folk music roots of grunge?"

## THE STUDY OF CHANGE IN ANTHROPOLOGY: CHALLENGES AND POSSIBILITIES

If this vignette is interesting to you, welcome to the world of culture change. When anthropology was founded a little more than a century ago, one of its chief concerns was how to study change among human populations. Anthropology frames change in at least two ways: the biological change that our species has experienced over time and the sociocultural changes that separate and define human populations in the present. A third issue for anthropologists interested in the variability of the human species, human culture, and society was how best to define the **scale** of their analysis. In other words, before we could study change, we had to establish a measure against which change could be studied effectively. Anthropologists continue to debate how best to study change, and we continue to debate just what the proper scale of our investigations should be. This essay offers a glimpse of some key issues and concerns for the field from the perspectives of those of us who study biological evolution and those who study sociocultural change.

We can talk about change in many different ways. To illustrate just how hard it is to talk about change, let us return to the opening vignette concerning music. Are we interested in the changes that your mother and father went through as their musical tastes developed from the Beatles to Beethoven? Alternatively, are we interested in how the music of your generation grew from the songs of your parents? Do we want to know why we find gamelan in Indonesia and not Western Europe? On the other hand, are we concerned with why all human populations make music? We might even ask whether humans are the only species on our planet that make music. What about the songs of birds and whales? Do these merit our interest?

Thus, there are various levels of complexity, different scales against which we want to talk about and investigate change. The first level focuses on individual changes, why you and your parents share different tastes. The second level focuses on historical patterns of change in the tastes of small groups. The third level posits questions that center on populations and asks where tastes sit in the social and cultural practices of a group. This would characterize the comment your mother made concerning the traditions of Western music and Indonesian gamelan, for example. Finally, the last level of analysis asks about human music in relation to other species and allows us to draw attention to the biological foundations of our behaviors.

## EARLY APPROACHES TO CHANGE

Early researchers interested in the processes of change in human populations assumed that biological and sociocultural changes were analogous and that human populations were divisible by geography or arbitrary markers such as skin color or technological standards. The scale of much early work was therefore a population, not a culture and certainly not the individual. **Social evolutionists,** including Herbert Spencer (1820–1903), argued that culture was a shared or universal attribute that evolved in a progressive, "ontogenetic" manner. Some cultures were infantile, whereas other cultures were quite mature (you can decide which level your music might fit). Because cultures evolved, they could be ranked according to their complexity, progress, and practices. Spencer used Victorian England as his ruler against which to measure most societies. He also argued that societies that did not "measure up" might catch up as they adopted the norms of English life. Models of "cultural evolution" were used to justify genocide against populations that were thought to be less evolved (biologically and culturally). Social evolutionists often borrowed Spencer's phrase "the survival of the fittest" and applied it to their analyses of culture. Cultures that could change and adapt would surely outlive and outperform those that were less evolved, or so thought social evolutionists.

Once again, let us return to our example of music. A social evolutionist would argue that the music you listen to is one indication of your culture's evolutionary status. Good music (in this case, classical music) is highly evolved. Your music (rock, rap, and grunge) is less evolved. Our interplanetary visitors would not hear major differences in musical styles; they are interested in universal patterns of behavior. In general, they would hear humans making music and ponder why so much of what they are hearing sounds the same.

If you think about this you will realize that the question is not just about how culture and society change over time. The question is also about the scale of those changes. The social evolutionists were interested in variations between groups that they defined in largely arbitrary and geographically limited ways (North Americans, Africans, and Europeans, for example). They associated moral values with each group and used each group to illustrate the various stages in their hierarchy of "cultural evolution," with Europeans at the top, Africans and Native Australians at the bottom. By the way, social evolutionists felt that most North Americans fit somewhere below Europeans because they lacked the benefits of life in the British Commonwealth. In any case, the social evolutionists created a model that not only ranked human cultures but also created a morally weighted measure of those ranks.

Lewis Henry Morgan (1818–1881), a North American lawyer and ethnographer of the Iroquois Indians, constructed an important hierarchical model that divided human populations into three groups. What Morgan called "savage populations" that had simple technology were put at the bottom of the system. "Barbarians" fit in the middle of the system and were more evolved than savages but still lacked the moral and ethical standards of "civilized" populations. Civilized populations sat at the top of Morgan's ranking system. Civilized society (by which Morgan meant Victorian England) was characterized by "high" moral standards, codified legal systems, well-defined leadership, and such details as private property, wealth, fine art, and, of course, fine music. In this kind of a system, a high score on the ladder is morally better (and more highly evolved) than a low score. Nevertheless, for the alien anthropologists, we are all just humans: a pre-intergalactic species of sentient carbon-based life forms made up mostly of water. On the alien scale, we rank somewhere above pond scum, but we probably would not even come close to the rank of a civilized and cultured population.

## HUMAN EVOLUTION AND BIOLOGICAL CHANGE

Today, we know that biological and sociocultural evolution are not the same and do not proceed in the same way. Culture does not follow biological logic, and biological evolution does not follow the progressive, directed path that can characterize sociocultural changes. How we know that has to do with the random nature of biological evolution is something we understand quite a bit better today than did the social evolutionists. Moreover, although biological evolution is a well-developed, technical subject, there are several basic concepts that you need to understand to appreciate the contrasts between biological and sociocultural change.

Victorian naturalist and scientist Charles Darwin (1809–1882) is most closely associated with our modern concept of biological evolution. However, it will not surprise you to learn that after a century and a half, we have a much better understanding of the process of evolution. Moreover, there no longer is any concern about finding evidence of the evolution of life on Earth. That is as undisputable as Newton's theory of gravitation or Boyle's theory of gases. Indeed, we now understand in detail how Darwin's evolution occurs and what its consequences are.

Parents transmit genes to offspring. Genes are made up of a unique molecule, DNA, the physical basis of heredity. Because chemical and physical systems are never perfect, new combinations of DNA occur randomly and spontaneously, like the unique snowflakes that fall outside your dorm during winter. You can think of DNA as a set of rules that help an organism become a reproductively active adult. Sometimes, variants of DNA enhance an organism's fitness; however, most variants have no effect, and some are lethal. In the long run, the accumulation of genetic variants is evolution. Note that although genes are a key cause of the development of anatomy, physiology, and behavior, the environment constantly interacts with the DNA by means of biochemical processes to determine who and what you are. Darwin based his theory of evolution on a mechanism of **cumulative selection.** In other words, he believed that evolution was the retention of fitness-enhancing traits and the elimination of traits that do not favor fitness over long periods. The result is **adaptation, speciation,** and the ever-branching tree of life.

We know now that selection does not drive all evolutionary change. Random processes, such as **mutation** and **drift,** cause changes in genes or gene frequencies in each generation that can alter the characteristics of organisms over time. Finally, the movement of genes between populations, **gene flow,** can also change the genetic and trait structure of a local population.

The important point to remember is that biological evolution, unlike sociocultural evolution, is the blind unfolding of particular physical and chemical systems in response to an ever-changing environment in which they are situated. It is mechanism, not creation. There is no agency, no goal, no progress, and no direction to this natural process. Although human hair color and height seem to be **adaptive responses** to the environment because of selection, we know that these traits vary from place to place and from time to time. Over generations, increased height and elongated limbs are better responses to the hot, arid, open habitats of sub-Saharan Africa than short stature and short limbs. However, when our human ancestors migrated out of Africa, they evolved different body forms in new habitats, such as the short and more compact body of Arctic peoples. On the other hand, diet, activity, stress, and a host of other environmental factors affect adult height. Over many generations (1,000 to 10,000), height, hair color, and other traits may change back and forth without any obvious trend. Adaptation is a response to the immediate, local environment. Over the long haul, evolution isn't going anywhere! Thus, evolution for biologists is any change in the genetic properties of a population over time, whether that change leads to a "better" organism or not.

Given these concepts from evolutionary biology, is "cultural evolution" at all like biological evolution? The short answer is "No." Go back to the questions concerning music, and in place of style think about the technology. How did your grandparents listen to a Beethoven symphony? They probably owned a series of thick, heavy, easily breakable, monophonic 78-rpm records. By the time your parents bought a Beethoven symphony, it was probably pressed on a single, stereophonic, 33-1/3-rpm, vinyl record. If you want to listen to a Beethoven symphony today, you might purchase a CD that includes three different versions of the same piece. Alternatively, you can download an MP3, without using any kind of disk.

## CULTURE CHANGE

Unlike biological evolution, social and cultural changes are driven by agents, human beings, who set goals and then act to reach them. In general, social and cultural changes are the result of conscious processes, and although we are not necessarily good at predicting the outcomes of change, because we learn norms from our parents, siblings, friends, and surroundings, we can learn how to make changes. The point is, unlike biological change that is largely random, we can talk about the progress that comes from sociocultural change. Comparing ten 78-rpm records with 5 megabytes on an MP3 player, you can clearly distinguish which is

better. It is important to remember that although we can plan for change in society, such changes are built on shared concepts of value and worth. You can ask
yourself why we would pursue social and cultural changes if we did not value
them. Nevertheless, this also means that points of disagreement will arise as
changes occur. Don't forget, your parents probably think your favorite music is
profoundly bad; in other words, it is not part of a progressive pattern of change. If
that gives you pause, just wait. When you have children, you'll probably feel the
same way about their favorite music.

Let us go a little farther with this point. Say you are a collector of 78-rpm
records. Are you less evolved because you enjoy the sound and ambience of the
recordings rather than the sterility of a modern MP3? This question returns us to
the crux of the problem when it comes to the study of change. What is the scale of
our investigations, and what are we hoping to learn?

American anthropologists reacted to social evolutionists in the early twentieth
century and quickly pointed out how inappropriate ranked models of human
social development were. One approach favored by North Americans was to follow how particular traits and practices diffused through a region; this approach
usually is described as **historical particularism** and is associated with anthropologists such as Franz Boas (1858–1942), Alfred Kroeber (1876–1960), and to a
lesser extent Margaret Mead (1901–1978). These anthropologists used collections
of material culture from an area to document how traits and practices developed.
They would ask, Where was a practice established? How was it adopted by other
cultures and populations? How did a trait change in its adoption? What they did
not care for were questions that focused on individual tastes. Thus, like their intergalactic counterparts, they were not interested in your musical tastes; instead,
they were interested in where your musical taste came from. To use their terminology, they were interested in knowing how patterns of use and tradition **diffused**
from one region to another. Historical particularists focused on how music moved
from one place to another. They would investigate why gamelan is found in
Indonesia and not Western Europe.

To get a better feel for how diffusion works, let's return to the example with
which we began. Music styles follow diffusional paths. One group borrows from
another and in the process creates something unique. Here is one example. Cohen
works in rural Mexico in the state of Oaxaca with a native population called the
Zapotec, a term that defines them by the language they speak. The pre-Hispanic
Zapotec, those who were around before the arrival of the Spanish, had music, but
they lacked instruments beyond forms of drums and flutes—at least that is what
we know from the archaeological record. Once the Spanish arrived, the Zapotec
(like most native groups) quickly adopted the instruments and musical traditions,
among other things, of their conquerors. They adapted the music of their conquerors to reflect their own interests. Today, you can purchase music sung in
Zapotec and played by native musicians on modern Western instruments. Sometimes they incorporate jazz and classical motifs. You can also find Western musicians who have borrowed from the Zapotec and sing in their language.

Other approaches have developed that replaced historical particularism and diffusional models through the twentieth century. Some anthropologists coped with the difficulties involved in studying change by ignoring it. **Structural functionalists** such as A. R. Radcliffe-Brown (1881–1955) were interested in how social systems maintained their status quo over time. A society was characterized as something like a car or a boat, and the key was to understand why a society would run smoothly over time like a boat and would not sink. Other anthropologists developed hierarchical models of social evolution that focused on technological change on one hand (e.g. Leslie White, 1900–1975) or argued that while societies evolved, that evolution took place at a local level and in a multitude of ways as local systems adapted to their particular ecologies (such as Julian Steward [1902–1972]). Although few scholars embraced the technological models of social evolution, the local evolutionary models are still with us under the heading of **cultural ecology.**

Anthropologists have gone off in a multitude of directions since the mid-twentieth century, founding symbolic, interpretive, postmodern, and economic approaches, among others. Nevertheless, how to deal with change continues to captivate the field. Many contemporary models of change approach the subject through an ethnographic lens. In other words, anthropologists use one of our key research tools, including **participant observation,** to understand the history, pattern, and process of change. By constructing ethnographic models of change, we are able to understand how a society or culture comes to appear as it does. We include historical data to understand why certain attributes may look the way they do. For example, a population's music may lack certain scales or particular instruments. We discover why the gaps are present through ethnographic research. Maybe it is a result of diffusion, or the lack of diffusion of a particular trait. Maybe a sociopolitical or socioeconomic event influenced the group, and one outcome was a change in musical traditions. Perhaps the issue is one of religion, and the society placed bans on certain types of musical expression, or perhaps only a certain type was encouraged. In any case, through careful ethnography anthropologists are able to trace patterns of change.

## SCALE AND CHANGE

The question of scale is crucial to the results of any study. Are we interested in a specific group? Do we want to know about one culture's practices? Alternatively, are we interested in intercultural variation? Maybe the question is one of gendered responses. For example, are there kinds of music made by men but not by women in your study population? Anthropologist Colin Turnbull spent many years with the BaMbuti of central Africa. He tells a story about how certain horns or flutes that are important in rituals to "calm the forest" for the BaMbuti became the property and responsibility of men. It seems that in the distant past, these horns or flutes originally belonged to women, but men stole them and hid them. As they claimed the horns and flutes from the women, men also claimed the mystical powers that were associated with the horns and flutes. The job for the anthropologist is to understand this example of change and why it is important. If you want to know more about this switch, you can read Turnbull's book *The Forest People*.

One point we have avoided is individual change and the question of why you like the particular music you like. Maybe you find yourself wondering, "How do I study individual change?" You might even think, "Well, I'm always changing, you know that line, I'm getting better every day in every way." You can complicate the question and add, "I'm the result of evolutionary process that is ongoing, so why aren't I evolving? Where does this leave me? How can I talk coherently about change? Where do I draw the line on what change is?"

## DO INDIVIDUALS EVOLVE?

This brings up another point that we want you to understand: when anthropologists talk about change, we are talking about changes that occur in populations, or groups of people. In fact, one of the points on which biological and sociocultural models tend to agree is that both areas are interested in changes that occur for a population, not for individuals. Think of it this way: populations evolve, and groups go through continuous sociocultural change. Individuals can change, too, but individuals do not evolve biologically. If you spent your life in a swimming pool, you would not grow webbed feet; nor would your children. You'd be wet, but you wouldn't change at a fundamental biological level. Nevertheless, if you wanted to live in water, you could adapt your sociocultural practices to facilitate the changes you wanted to make. For the anthropologist you might be interesting but not a good subject for study, unless of course you convince lots of people to join you and live under water. What the individual does is interesting, but from an anthropological perspective we don't tend to focus on individual tastes except in how they illustrate group norms. We use ethnographic fieldwork and genetics to focus on populations, and we work with individuals to understand the range of the patterns that we hope to define. We are able to control and cut through the background noise and variation that characterize individual patterns by studying and talking about change in terms of populations.

## CULTURAL RELATIVISM AND CHANGE

The ranking and subjectivity that characterized the social evolutionists still haunt much work on culture change. It is extremely hard not to judge and measure a population's sociocultural systems against our own. For example, suppose the alien anthropologists choose you to visit their world and to listen to their music in an effort to conduct a comparative study of the two populations. You step off the ramp leading from the wormhole transportation system and realize that you are hungry. You want a pizza. "Pizza?" your hosts ask, "What is pizza? How about these lovely tubeworms we eat lightly tossed in a rich sesame sauce?" The aliens like to eat the worms raw, but they are trying to be nice. This might seem a trivial illustration, but the point is important. It is extremely hard to study a foreign society or cultural system without judging that system.

Some anthropologists argue that in such a situation, you must exercise complete **cultural relativism,** and they are mostly correct. Cultural relativism asks anthropologists and investigators to try to put aside their own cultural beliefs and social rules and to try to understand what is happening around them from a native's perspective. Cultural relativism is hard to manage. What if you need to spend a year with the aliens? For an entire year, everything you've grown up with is missing: your favorite foods, your favorite movies, your favorite music. Moreover, all that time, you have to try your best to understand what is going on from the native's point of view. This is what anthropologists do to understand society and culture. Getting beyond our sociocultural biases is one of the reasons we do fieldwork. The goal is to understand society and culture from the native's perspective. Given this, we want to make one point clear: being culturally relative does not mean we are morally relative. In other words, a cultural relativist doesn't say, "Anything goes!" We will leave moral relativism for the philosophers to debate. However, as you learn about cultures and societies from around the world (and maybe someday from other worlds), we want you to remain as open-minded as you can and to work hard to limit the amount of ranking and valuation.

## A LAST EXAMPLE AND THOUGHT

Let's proceed to an example of cultural change. We started this chapter by asking what kind of music you like, and now we will return to music. Do you like the same kind of music that you liked when you were in grade school or high school? Would you describe your taste in music as changing over time? Has your taste improved? In addition, why has your taste changed? Have you heard new genres of music or new artists? The kinds of changes that characterize how your taste in music develops probably seem quite progressive. Maybe you would describe the music you listen to today as more complex than the music you listened to as a child.

In fact, changing tastes in music can be directional. In other words, you can learn to like a new kind of music. You can even take a very active role in exposing yourself to new music. However, the change can also be random and arbitrary. You are walking across campus and you hear something different coming from a dorm window. You find out what it is, and there you are a random act of change! Change in this case can be random or directional, but your parents might not think it is progressive.

Add a layer of complication to the question of cultural change. We know that you like a certain kind of music. You know how your tastes have changed. However, if we are interested in cultural patterns, how can we cut through the fact that no two people share the exact same tastes in music? Use yourself as an example: do you share the exact same tastes in music as your friends? If we want to get deeply philosophical, we can ask, "How do you know you even hear the music the same?"

Anthropologists resolve the problem of individual variation in a couple of different ways. First, we never talk to only one person. Instead, we take a sample of a group of people and call those people our **informants**. There might be one extremely useful informant, a key informant, but if we are worth our weight in ethnography, we will talk to a representative, random sample of a group. By talking to a random group that is representative of a population, we are more likely to hear about a good deal of the variation that is present in a population. We can also use the responses of a random group of informants to understand where people agree and disagree about cultural practices.

We hope that this brief review of how anthropologists study change and why biological and sociocultural changes are different has been useful. We want to encourage you to practice what you have learned: look around you and think about how patterns change over time. From food to clothing to music, there is an amazing amount to study: you can design your own diffusional models of music or clothing, or maybe the spread of pizza and bagels from East Coast cities such as New York to the entire country. You don't need to go to some foreign setting for this to be interesting; just think of how slang moves across our country. That is a diffusional study of culture change you can do from your desk. But don't stop with the easy stuff; think about the tough issues, too. Why do humans tend to want to associate biological and sociocultural evolution when they have such different processes? Why are social evolutionary models so persuasive, and why have these models been used to promote hatred? These are tough questions, but they are questions that we must answer.

# Why Do Anthropological Experts Disagree?

ANNE CAMPBELL, *Washington State University*

PATRICIA C. RICE, *West Virginia University*

What image comes to mind when you hear the name Ozzy Osbourne? Do you see a middle-aged dad who doesn't quite "get it" or a hard rock icon who shocked the world when he bit the head off a bat during a concert?[1] Do you think Ozzy's children are awesome, or are they awful, defiant brats? Are *Grand Theft Auto* 1, 2, and 3 great video games or a threat to society because they teach children to steal cars and encourage criminal behavior? Is the TV series *Buffy the Vampire Slayer* ridiculous because it is based on things that don't exist, is it cute and somewhat thoughtful, or is it an extraordinary blend of art and modern life, a "balance of mythic power and postmodern self-consciousness" (Wilcox 2002)? Did woolly mammoths talk, and if they did, did they sound like Ray Romano? The answers to these questions depend on the age, sex, and previous experience of individual consumers of "popular culture." Whereas 3- to 5-year-olds would agree after seeing *Ice Age* that woolly mammoths did talk, even speaking English, and made dandy pets, adults would not. And whereas most teenagers might think the *Buffy* series is cute, most adults probably don't. And there is probably no consensus on the phenomenon called Ozzy Osbourne relative to categories related to sex, age, or previous experience.

Cultural anthropologists, who specialize in analyzing cultural phenomena in their own and in other cultures are also involved in analyzing the cultural context of Ozzy, Buffy, or wooly mammoths. But instead of only having biases based on their age, sex, or previous experiences, cultural anthropologists also have biases based on how they interpret cultural phenomena, and they would probably not agree with each other on any of the questions posed earlier. Why not?

What image comes to mind when you hear the word "Neandertal"? Do you imagine a slouching, hairy beast, wearing a bedraggled animal skin with one shoulder bare, with a club in one hand, dragging a woman by her hair into a cave, saying "ugh" all the while? Although we cannot view Neandertal directly, we have fossils that might indicate a slouched posture or speech, and we have artifacts that might indicate that they had clubs or tools that could be used to scrape animal hides for clothing. Biological anthropologists and archaeologists have to interpret those fossil and artifactual materials, and they do not necessarily agree on those interpretations. Why not?

As a start, Thomas Kuhn, the leading philosopher of science in the mid-1900s, wrote that what people see depends on what they look at and what their "previous visual and conceptual experience has taught" them to see (1962:111). That statement is as true today as when Kuhn wrote it 40 years ago. What we look at is not the same as what we see. This observation explains in part why anthropological experts disagree.

To understand the difference between looking and seeing, mentally put an apple on the table in front of you and mentally invite two friends to observe that apple with you. ("Observation" is used here as a neutral term.) Don't talk about the apple; you may walk around it but cannot pick it up or manipulate it. Take 5 minutes to write down your observations and then compare notes with your two friends.

Did you all write down a color? Was it the same color and in the same detail? Did you compare the color with a formal color chart? Did you recognize what kind of apple it is? Did you all observe size and if so, did you say the same thing about its size? Probably not. Some of you observed color, but maybe not all; some may have matched its color with a color chart, but others probably just noted a generic term, "red" or "green." Some probably noted that it was a MacIntosh or a Delicious, but others didn't. In short, no two people will see the same things or ask the same questions, much less use the same methods to attempt to find answers. Looking at the apple is one thing; seeing it involves using what Kuhn calls "visual-conceptual experience."

Now ask yourself, "Because we were all looking at the same thing, why didn't we all see the same thing?" If you had been allowed to discuss the investigation beforehand, you all might have agreed on what to observe, what questions to ask, and even what methods would be best to use to ask them, but you were not allowed to do that. Some obvious answers to the "Why did you differ question" might be that one friend is a horticulture major and knows apple variety names by merely looking at them and the rest of you don't, one of you is a fashion design major and is particularly experienced in differentiating colors, and one of you is a math major and used to assessing size. Female observers might be more interested in color, male observers might be more interested in size, older observers might be more interested in the variety, and younger observers might be interested only in eating the apple. Obviously, previous experience is an important variable in terms of what each of you observed and saw, but so are age and sex. These are all variables that resulted in bias, assumptions, and preconceptions that changed what you looked at to what you saw. They were the lens between the reality of the apple and what you each saw. And these same variables are part of the reason why anthropologists disagree with each other on scientific issues.

## BIAS, SCIENCE, AND ANTHROPOLOGY

It does not matter whether a scientist is a physicist, biologist, geologist, or anthropologist, and it does not matter whether the anthropologist is a cultural anthropologist, a biological anthropologist, or an archaeologist; these same variables will cause at least some bias in the investigation of any scientific arena. Male scientists and female scientists are not necessarily interested in answering the same questions about the same phenomenon because they don't necessarily see them as having equal importance; their sex alone may affect the questions they ask and the methods of inquiry they use. In the case of cultural anthropologists, sex may also influence the kind of data to which they have access. Older and younger scientists are not necessarily interested in answering the same questions in the same ways, either. And one's past experience is always an important variable in regard to the questions asked and methods used. These differences explain in part why experts disagree.

Another variable that leads to bias is inherent in the nature of science. Early scientists assumed that they were capable of clearing their minds of all preconceptions and bias and achieving total objectivity. As a result, they believed great "truths" of science would emerge at the end of their investigations. These early scientists believed there was a real world out there that could be observed and seen directly, and they went about doing science with that belief in mind (Chamberlain and Hartwig 1999; Clark 1993). These early scientists are called strict empiricists. Although some scientists still believe they are unbiased, strict empiricism was and is a myth. Sex, age, and individual experience will always influence what humans see and do.

By the early twentieth century, most scientists operated under the belief that there still was a real world out there but that it could not be observed or seen directly; additionally, they believed that what they observed had to be interpreted and therefore would always be somewhat biased, but they believed that precise data collecting, hypothesis generating, and appropriate testing would yield results that would be as close as they could come to "reality" and "true knowledge" about the world. Philosophers of science call these scientists logical positivists (Binford and Sabloff 1982). Thomas Kuhn believes this is how most scientists actually do science today, suggesting that scientists "get in the middle" of their science, whether they want to or not and whether they realize it or not (Chamberlain and

Hartwig 1999). Most scientists probably would grudgingly agree with this perspective, and it is the one taken here: scientists attempt to be as unbiased as they can, but preconceptions, assumptions, subjectivity, and bias are always present in one form or another and to one extent or another. (Some modern scientists do not believe there is a real world out there at all to discover. Some believe there are numerous worlds out there, not just one. And some believe that one or more worlds can't be discovered well enough to even try. These critical theory advocates are in the minority and are regarded by many as being highly critical of other scientists but as not having advanced science using their philosophy. They will not be discussed further.)

## INTELLECTUAL TRADITIONS, CULTURE, AND PARADIGMS

To get back to the question of why experts disagree on anthropological issues, differences in sex, age, and individual experience are at least partially the cause of the subjective lens through which they view their world. There is an additional anthropological bias, called the **intellectual tradition,** that is also behind how we interpret what we observe. The intellectual tradition bias is stronger in paleo-anthropology (archaeology, prehistory, and human evolution) than in cultural anthropology, although cultural anthropology has not escaped different ways to conceptualize culture.

The two intellectual traditions that have arisen in Western science that affect anthropology exist for historical reasons going back to the last quarter of the nineteenth century (Clark and Willermet 1995). What is called the Old World (OW) tradition exists in England and on the European continent and has its intellectual roots mainly in history, nationalism, and natural sciences, but also, depending on the anthropological specialty, in geology, paleontology, and sociology. What is called the New World (NW) tradition exists in America and has its roots in Native American cultural studies that existed at the time anthropology became a discipline in the United States a little more than a hundred years ago. Under the OW tradition, most British and European anthropologists see human evolution and human prehistory as history projected into the preliterate past, with the processes that cause human evolution and culture change being the same as today. Under this tradition, most cultural anthropologists see modern "other cultures" as different from their own and focus on finding and explaining those differences. By contrast, under the NW tradition, most American anthropologists see human evolution and prehistory as entities in their own right; most cultural anthropologists see modern "other cultures" as they exist in our backyards as Native Americans and focus on finding and explaining the similarities that exist in all cultures (Binford and Sabloff 1982; Clark 1993).

Experts learn their particular tradition as they learn their science; obviously, which tradition an expert learns and supports depends on the side of the Atlantic

Ocean on which he or she is trained. In anthropology, students take a first anthropology course, choose to pursue it as a career, and begin to unconsciously pick up some of the intellectual tradition of the instructor. And the students continue to be immersed in this single tradition (usually without knowing it), so that by the time they have earned their Ph.D. degrees and are ready to begin their careers, they are steeped in that tradition.

One of the major reasons why OW and NW intellectual traditions differ is because each views the concept of culture somewhat differently. Beginning in the 1800s, with the development of the social sciences, OW anthropologists regarded "a culture" and "cultures" as being the same as "a people" and "peoples," each having its own unique and internally consistent package of material objects such as clothing and food, language, and physical type. Indeed, under the OW tradition, experts think of "the English People" as a homogeneous group of people wearing similar clothing and eating "bangers, mash, and boiled cabbage," all speaking the Queen's English, and all being tall and light skinned, with light brown hair. The fact that this stereotype is not very accurate is beside the point. The point is that under this tradition, "a people" connotes a multifaceted unit of language, culture, and biology, all tied together as a neat package. Along with this view go ideas that logically stem from this OW view of culture: associated traits (material objects and functionally related biological traits) constantly occur together, but blending or mixing of traits does not occur. When change occurs, it does so rapidly as if one "people" somehow replaced another (punctuated equilibrium), and the result over time and space is **discontinuity** in both biology and culture (Clark 1993; 2002).

By contrast, NW anthropologists view culture as being above and larger than the level of social, ethnic, and linguistic groups and as made up of different traits (material objects and biological traits) that are not and were not necessarily always associated with each other. Traits and complexes can occur in many areas, and the blend or mix of traits is common and to be expected. Change usually occurs gradually as inventions and shared ideas add up, but when there is rapid change, it is caused by a change in environment (Darwinian gradualism); finally, the result over time and space is **continuity** in both biology and culture (Clark 1993; 2002).

If preconceptions, subjectivity, and bias (due to sex, age, and previous experiences) are added to intellectual tradition, the result is what is called a **paradigm** (Clark 1993). A paradigm includes the sum of the different biases scientists have between reality and what the scientist sees as well as the intellectual tradition the scientist has grown up with and defends. A paradigm is a kind of frame through which the scientist views his or her world and as such is logically consistent. Paradigms usually are called by the name of their intellectual tradition, but remember that paradigms also include the collective bias taken to the scientific table. Paradigm differences are the consummate reason why experts disagree even when there are the same things to see.

## PARADIGMS IN CULTURAL ANTHROPOLOGY

Paradigms influence how one conceptualizes what one is going to study. They also influence the methods by which data are documented. For example, cultural anthropologists gather data by observation. However, what they see and how they interpret it depends in part on the paradigm through which they view the world. For example, consider the concept of culture. In 1952, Alfred Kroeber and Clyde Kluckhohn reviewed hundreds of published articles and books and identified 164 different concepts and definitions of culture, as developed by social scientists in the previous several decades. The following definition was their synthesis of the critical concepts presented in those 164 definitions:

> Culture consists of patterns, explicit and implicit, of and for behavior acquired and transmitted by symbols, constituting the distinctive achievement of human groups, including their embodiments in artifacts. The essential core of culture consists of traditional (i.e., historically derived and selected) ideas and especially their attached values; culture systems may on the one hand, be considered as products of action, on the other hand as conditioning elements of further action. (p. 181)

Using this definition of culture, anthropologists could study the same cultural event and focus on different components identified in the definition. Depending on which aspects were emphasized, the anthropologists could gather data that would result in different interpretations of group behavior or different understandings of the cultural significance of that event. For example, if an anthropologist were interested in power relationships and change and focused data collection on cultural institutions and their interrelationships, he or she might not pay attention to child-rearing practices that could have provided insight into the cultural transmission of belief systems that reinforce and reproduce the existing power structures. Conversely, if the anthropologist focused on child-rearing practices, he or she might not realize their implications for the maintenance of the status quo within the larger society. Does this make either data set inaccurate or incomplete, or are they different descriptions of different qualities of the same "apple" called culture? As experts attempt to answer this question, they will probably disagree.

In addition to these issues, experts may disagree on the interpretation of particular data. One reason is that the interpretation is often made in light of **theories** that are constructed to attempt to explain the larger paradigm in which the anthropologists were trained and through which they view the world. (See Chapter 4 for more discussion of theories.) In the late 1800s, for example, cultural anthropologists shared the belief "that evolution meant human progress from primitive (savage) through an intermediate (barbarian) to a civilized stage" (Goodenough 2002:427). This "progress" was thought to be universal, and interpretations of cultural data were used to develop theories of cultural differences that fit that belief. J. Boggs (2002) argues that remnants of this paradigm can still be seen in contemporary debates regarding U.S. policy toward Native Americans. Throughout the twentieth century, the theories that guided cultural anthropologists changed as different generations gained knowledge and insights regarding human behavior. With these changes have come debates between experts who adhere to different theories. Debates include discussions of the adequacy of data gathered, the accuracy of the theory as a tool to interpret the cultural change, and the value of findings and interpretations as contributions to our overall understanding of the human condition.

Adequacy of the data depends in part on the representativeness of the events that cultural anthropologists observe and in which they participate. One cannot document well what one cannot see or experience, and one cannot document at all the elements of culture that one does not even know exist. It is here that age and gender play a key role in understanding why experts disagree.

Because of their sex and age, anthropologists may not be aware of or have access to critical cultural information and events. Both of these factors are illustrated in Diane Freedman's work in Romania (1986). She began her study of dance and gender roles as a married woman and was able to document the roles and norms pertinent to that status. Through her husband's activities and his interaction with the men, she gained access to the men's perspective as well. When she returned to her fieldwork after the death of her husband, her status changed to that of widow. This change gave her access to another dimension of female gender roles, that of caretaker for the ill and dying. Older widows in the community with whom she had little contact when she was married wanted to learn of her experiences and in turn shared theirs, as well as their perspectives on death. When Freedman's period of mourning ended during her fieldwork, her status changed overnight to one of single, eligible woman. This change made it possible for her to interact with young unmarried women and to participate in activities appropriate for that group. She was able to learn "about customs and spells for attracting men as husbands and dance partners" (1986: 351), knowledge and activities to which she had had limited or no access in her prior statuses as wife and widow.

Sex also affects the importance given to cultural events and the ways in which those events are interpreted. This influence can be seen in differences between male and female perspectives within a community. It can also be seen in a comparison of ethnographies written by male and female anthropologists who have studied the same cultural group. In *Headhunter's Heritage,* for example, Robert Murphy (1960) documents in detail the Mundurucu culture (Amazonia) through the lens of male activities and ideology. Only 10 of the 193 pages are devoted to a discussion of women and family. The concept of gossip receives a paragraph and is characterized as "the chief form of expression of antagonism among the women" (116–17). In *Women of the Forest,* Yolanda and Robert Murphy (1985) examine the differences between the women and men's perspectives, and more than 160 pages detail aspects of the women's world not found in Robert's previous work. For example, Yolanda learned through her interactions with the women that gossip plays several essential roles in the social life of the community. First, it provides "valuable information about people, . . . events in other communities, and nearly every other subject conceivable in their restricted worlds" (159–60). It also is an informal indicator of importance within the group: "it may be worrisome for a Mundurucu woman to know she is being talked about, but it would be a disaster if she were to discover that nobody was talking about her" (160). Yolanda documented the hostile uses of gossip, but she found that negative gossip that focused on sexual exploits was done for a reason. Sexual promiscuity threatened the "moral solidarity of the females." Rather than being just an indicator of antagonism between women, it was in fact a powerful "negative sanction exercised by women over their wayward member to bring her back into line before the men staged a gang rape" (160–61). Gossip thus provided women with an important means for timely intervention designed to prevent extreme punishment for the violation of cultural norms. The influence of sex on differences in data gathered and interpreted, as illustrated by the Murphys' work, provides insights into some of the reasons why experts disagree.

## PARADIGMS IN PALEOANTHROPOLOGY

Paleoanthropology is defined as the science of humans in the past: biological anthropology concentrates on human evolution, and archaeology concentrates on human prehistory. Because the world's scientists do not have a time machine to use to go back to prehistoric times and places to view paleocultures in action (as cultural anthropologists can do today) or see what populations were interbreeding with other populations (as modern biologists can), common sense suggests that there is a large and fertile ground for disagreement among paleoanthropologists. Under the OW paradigm, most European and British paleoanthropologists view the human past as being made up of people living in distinct groups that were homogeneous in material traits, language, and biology and that did not mix with other groups, and when biological or cultural change occurred, it was quick in time and space because of invasions or replacements. The emphasis is on discontinuity. Most OW paleoanthropologists emphasize differences in material objects and morphology and give a separate name to each population in time or space. This is called **splitting**. By contrast, under the NW paradigm, most American paleoanthropologists view the human past as being made up of people living in groups that met up with other groups deliberately for mating purposes or accidentally when their hunting territories overlapped; they exchanged ideas, material items, and genes in the process, and when change occurred, it was slow and continuous through time and small between groups living at the same time. The emphasis is on continuity. NW paleoanthropologists emphasize similarities in material objects and morphology and lump populations together under single names (Clark 1993).

Let us now focus on one ongoing controversy in paleoanthropology and put intellectual traditions together with biases (that is, paradigms) to try to discover why experts on the two sides of the Atlantic disagree over this single issue. The controversy is over the position of Neandertal in the evolution of modern humans. Basically, the question is, "Did Neandertal have anything to do with our ancestry?" The OW paradigm claims they were not in our ancestry. OW proponents agree that there was an apparent 10,000-year overlap of the two populations living in the Near East and in Europe—the last 10,000 years of Neandertal and the first 10,000 years of modern humans—but they firmly believe that the two populations did not interbreed[2] or exchange material objects. These experts conclude that the two groups did not influence each other culturally, linguistically, or biologically, that there was no intermingling or hybridization, and that change (that is, the demise of Neandertal at about 30,000 years ago) came quickly. These experts assign the term *Homo neandertalensis* rather than *Homo sapiens* (for modern humans) to demonstrate their belief in discontinuity, splitting, and separate species status. All of these points make logical sense once the paradigm is understood.

By contrast, the NW paradigm claims Neandertal did have a role to play in the evolution of modern humans, with proponents suggesting that the two populations were interbreeding, although how much is difficult to ascertain. These experts conclude that the two populations did influence each other by exchanging material objects and ideas as well as genes, and that change—the demise of Neandertal—was primarily through interbreeding, with both archaeological and biological Neandertal traits slowly disappearing by 30,000 years ago. These experts assign the term *Homo sapiens neandertalensis* to the Neandertal population, confirming their belief in continuity and only subspecies status. Again, this makes logical sense once the paradigm is understood.

Now you know why experts differ on the Neandertal question, and the stage is set for proponents in each paradigm to do science. But experts from each paradigm ask different questions, look at different data, use different methods, take different measurements, and come to different conclusions. Additionally, experts accuse the other "side" of using bad, fragmentary, or incorrect data, using bad methods, being contradictory and misinformed, coming up with wrong conclusions, and not understanding the other side. Proponents of each paradigm also say they have tested their paradigm and found it to be superior to the other at answering the question and claim that the other side just can't see it (Smith and Harrold 1997). As one example, let's look at data and measurements. In 1997 Cathy Willermet looked at the thirty-nine publications written during the previous 15 years by experts supporting one or the other paradigms and found that when 680 data points representing sixty-one variables were taken on fifty-five Neandertal fossils, only 11 percent of the measurements were used by both sides, leaving 89 percent of the data essentially not usable (Clark and Willermet 1997). The choice of fossils used in analysis and the weight given each trait also vary between the supporters of the two paradigms. Additionally, in paleoanthropology, the dates of fossil and artifact data are vital to answering any question, and unfortunately the best dating technique (carbon-14 in this case) is at the extreme end (40,000 years ago) of its accuracy, so when conflicting dates are given, the one chosen often depends on how well it fits a particular paradigm.

Under these circumstances, it is no wonder that a British expert, steeped in "culture as a people," probably will see discontinuity between Neandertal and modern humans and see separate species status. By contrast, it is no wonder that an American expert probably will see continuity between Neandertal and modern humans and see only subspecies status. And this is generally the way it is. Even though these experts have access to the same fossil and artifactual data, some look at the data through the lens of the OW paradigm and some through the NW paradigm. With few exceptions, British and European paleoanthropologists claim Neandertal was not part of our ancestry, and with the same few exceptions, American paleoanthropologists claim that Neandertal was involved in our ancestry. When new data and even new kinds of data are introduced, proponents of each side interpret them as supporting only their paradigm.

Under these circumstances, it is also understandable why François Bordes, France's leading archaeologist in the mid-1900s, decided that the entire collection of Neandertal flint tools in Europe and the Middle East, which he called Mousterian industries, could be classified into four types (called facies, each with a name) based on absence or presence and the frequency of numerous kinds of tools (Bordes 1968). Although these four types were not located in four distinct areas or in four chronological time periods, he still maintained that they represented four tribal groups that did not interact with each other. One could envision four independent peoples wandering Europe and the Middle East for thousands of years without exchanging tool recipes or genes or even being able to say "Hi" in passing. Bordes viewed prehistoric Europe through the OW paradigm. Given his reputation, his scheme was accepted until Lewis Binford, an American archaeologist, questioned the four-tribe notion. The argument over whether the four categories represent four cultural groups or four tool functions came to a standstill in the mid-1960s. Which answer you choose to believe depends on your paradigm (Clark 2002).

A final "why" question is in order here: "Why does each side continue to adhere so strongly to its paradigm?" Consider the following possibility. In the last two hundred years, Europe has seen many conflicts on its land, from world wars to continent-wide wars to internal wars, and has seen entire populations— "peoples" in the OW culture, language, and biology package—being physically moved many miles away or being exterminated, with other populations coming in and displacing original populations, over and over again. This history reinforces discontinuity as the norm in the OW. By contrast, America has not seen such turmoil. The two world wars were not fought on American soil, the Civil War did not displace entire populations, and although there has been much immigration of people from the rest of the world, whole populations were not moved or replaced because of it. It is easier to think of continuity, the exchange of ideas and genes, and a resultant "melting pot" as the norm in the NW (Clark 1993).

## CONCLUSION

So where do we and should we stand as anthropologists relative to science in general, paradigms, the Neandertal question, and cultural disagreements? Kuhn is correct that scientists operate with bias and subjectivity, knowingly or unknowingly, because each is a member of only one sex, is at a certain age in life, has had unique experiences, and has been brought up in only one intellectual tradition; therefore, each scientist views science through a single paradigm, one that does not necessarily agree with other scientists' paradigms, and that causes disagreement. As for existing paradigms in any discipline such as anthropology, Kuhn predicts that they will not change quickly. In regard to the Neandertal question, several scientists not directly involved in the controversy have suggested that the two paradigms will continue until the major proponents of each side have died. But even then, their many students will carry on the fight just because of entrenched positions. Each side has proponents who seem to think that if they yell louder and more often than the other side, they will win the argument. Although new fossil and artifact data and correct dates for all of the materials are welcome, they will be evaluated by each side in terms of its preferred paradigm and will not solve the paradigm dilemma.

That experts disagree seems to be a theme that permeates anthropology in general. Cultural anthropologists are no more in agreement about cultural phenomena and how to interpret them than paleoanthropologists are in interpreting past human events. It may not be something we are proud of, but it is a commonality. And disagreement is common to any endeavor that attempts to be scientific; it comes with the territory. As a former president of the American Anthropological Association, James Peacock, wrote in 1986, "many anthropologists would deny that there is any overriding perspective [guiding all anthropological inquiry;] . . . many anthropologists seek some unifying perspective" (p. 93). The one thing all anthropologists have in common is a search for knowledge about the human condition, past and present, biologically and culturally. A second commonality is that in our search for knowledge, we can–and must–disagree.

## NOTES

1. The authors have been told several different stories about whether the bat was real or plastic, live or dead. We will leave it at that.
2. Some OW experts admit there might have been a bit of interbreeding but believe it was unimportant and had no effect on either population.

## REFERENCES

BINFORD, L. R. and J. A. SABLOFF
    1982. "Paradigms, Systematics and Archaeology." *Journal of Anthropological Research* 38(2):137–53.
BOGGS, J.
    2002. "Anthropological Knowledge and Native American Cultural Practice in the Liberal Polity." *American Anthropologist* 104(2):598–610.
BORDES, F.
    1968. *The Old Stone Age.* New York: McGraw-Hill.

CHAMBERLAIN, J. G. and W. C. HARTWIG
   1999. "Thomas Kuhn and Paleoanthropology." *Evolutionary Anthropology* 8(2):42–45.

CLARK, G. A.
   1993. "Paradigms in Science and Archaeology." *Journal of Archaeological Research* 1(3):203–29.
   2002. "Neandertal Archaeology: Implications for Our Origins." *American Anthropologist* 104(1):50–67.

CLARK, G. A. and C. WILLERMET
   1995. "Paradigm Crisis in Modern Human Origin Research." *Journal of Human Evolution* 29:487–90.

CLARK, G. A. and C. WILLERMET, eds.
   1997. *Conceptual Issues in Recent Modern Human Origins.* New York: Aldine de Gruyter.

FREEDMAN, D.
   1986. "Wife, widow, Woman: Roles of an Anthropologist in a Transylvania Village." In Peggy Golde, ed. *Women in the Field,* (2nd edition). Berkeley CA: University of California Press. pp. 333–58.

GOODENOUGH, W.
   2002. "Anthropology in the 20th Century and Beyond." *American Anthropologist* 104(2):423–40.

KROEBER, A. and C. KLUCKHOHN
   1952. "Culture: A Critical Review of Concepts and Practices." *Papers of the Peabody Museum of American Archaeology and Ethnology,* Vol 47. Cambridge, MA: Harvard University Press.

KUHN, THOMAS
   1962. *The Structure of Scientific Revolutions.* Chicago: University of Chicago Press.

MURPHY, R.
   1960. *Headhunter's Heritage: Social and Economic Change among the Mundurucu Indians.* Berkeley: University of California Press.

MURPHY, Y. and R. MURPHY
   1985. *Women of the Forest* (2nd edition). New York: Columbia University Press.

PEACOCK, J.
   1986. *The Anthropological Lens.* New York: Cambridge University Press.

SMITH, S. L. and F. B. HARROLD
   1997. "A Paradigm's Worth of Difference? Understanding the Impasse over Modern Human Origins." *Yearbook of Physical Anthropology* 40:113–38.

WILCOX, R.
   2002. *Fighting the Forces: What's at Stake in Buffy the Vampire Slayer.* Lanham, MD: Rowman & Littlefield.

# Thinking and Acting Ethically in Anthropology

ANN KINGSOLVER, *University of South Carolina*

If you take a philosophy class on ethics, you might be discussing Jean-Paul Sartre's (1948:40) description of a student's dilemma (Should he join the resistance against fascism or continue taking care of his mother?), or you might be considering the arguments for and against euthanasia or abortion.[1] When we talk about ethics in anthropology, we narrow the scope of the questions to apply to the practice of our discipline. However, ethics always involves asking questions of yourself and others, and making decisions, usually about what will be the least harmful course of action. For example, if an archaeologist encounters human remains while digging test pits for the highway department to see whether there is any evidence of occupation by earlier groups, should the archaeologist notify someone? If so, who should be notified? Should the archaeologist continue with the excavation or stop and cover it back over, including the human remains? What laws and professional codes guide archaeologists in making such a decision? How is this an ethical problem? When we talk about human rights, does this include respecting the rights of dead people and their descendants? Are all dead people treated equally?

What thinking anthropologically and thinking ethically have in common is this: we try to consider as many perspectives as possible with regard to whatever we are studying or whatever problems we are attempting to solve. Usually, that means actively seeking others' points of view on an issue because we cannot see all possible ramifications of an action from our own perspectives. Different cultures may have different logics, for example, when it comes to ethical decision-making, and because anthropology may involve cross-cultural communication and study, it may take teamwork to decide what would be the most beneficial process for all who might be affected by anthropological research. Asking questions is a very important, active part of acting ethically in anthropology. Rather than simply learning a list of "dos and don'ts" in the discipline, anthropological ethics involves learning how to ask questions that are well informed by past experiences, professional guidelines, and the laws, policies, and cultural preferences of those in whose regions we work. As a student of anthropology, you not only have a responsibility to think and act ethically along with the professionals, you also have rights as specified in the American Anthropological Association's Code of Ethics.

In this chapter, I will talk about why ethics matter in anthropology, including ethics in the classroom. I will provide examples of the way anthropologists keep learning from our mistakes, creating and revising ethical codes that are meant to guide (but are unable to sanction) behavior by fellow anthropologists. Specific topics addressed in courses on anthropological ethics that will be summarized briefly in this chapter include informed consent; human rights; cultural and ethical relativism; the U.S. Native American Graves Protection and Repatriation Act (NAGPRA) of 1990; intellectual, biological, and other property rights; whistleblowing; ethical issues in the collection and representation of data; visual ethics; insider and outsider research issues; equity issues inside and outside universities; conflicts in accountability; and collaborative decision-making.

Anthropological learning implies contracts of **respect** on several levels. Professional anthropologists, whether working in academic or other contexts, are bound by personal and professional ethics to respect those with whom we work, living or dead, at home (wherever home may be) or in another region. In turn, as you learn about the cultural, linguistic, biological, historical, and prehistoric aspects of human experience from what professional anthropologists (including archaeologists) are learning, you enter into that contract of respect as well. For example, if you see a film in class that was made by an anthropologist, the practice of professional ethics means that the maker of that film obtained (or should have obtained) the consent of those being filmed to have their images and words studied by you and others. When consent is negotiated, as I will explain later in this chapter, the anthropologist explains the project as fully as possible. The agreement made between the filmmaker and those filmed is entered into, by extension, by the person showing you the film and by you, the viewer. As an undergraduate, then, you are acting as a professional anthropologist when you view a film with respect for those portrayed, no matter how different their life experience may be from your own.

If you participate in a research exercise as part of a course in any subfield of anthropology in the United States, and that exercise involves human subjects (for example, talking with people outside your classroom as part of an assignment), then you are also acting as a professional anthropologist and you are bound by national legislation to carry out that research in an ethically responsible way. On campuses and in communities, there are Institutional Review Boards made up of people from various backgrounds who review research proposals and classroom exercises that involve human subjects and decide whether they might cause harm to those being asked to participate in the research. This is why, if you are conducting a life history interview or taping and transcribing a conversation, you should give the person you interview a description of your project and contact information and obtain his or her consent before you begin the interview. Hiding a tape recorder and taping a conversation without consent not only is unethical and unanthropological but it can also cause an institution to lose federal funding. **Informed consent** means that a person knows as much as he or she can about the purpose of the research project in which he or she agrees to participate, the methods used, and the dissemination of results, and agrees to work with the researcher by voluntarily signing a consent form or giving verbal consent on an audiotape or videotape. The researcher is responsible for explaining the project clearly, respecting the collaborator's (a name for the person agreeing to participate in the research) wishes regarding anonymity or other stipulations, and providing the person who is helping or teaching the anthropologist with the results of the project. You can find guidelines for informed consent, and the entire Code of Ethics, on the American Anthropological Association's Web site (aaanet.org).

One basic ethical guideline to remember is that whereas journalists are accountable to the public (providing the full story), anthropologists are accountable to those we ask to provide us with their time and knowledge. This may sometimes mean that the ethical thing to do is to *not* tell the full story. For example, if naming ancestors is culturally forbidden and documenting a family history violates the contract of respect an anthropologist has with his or her collaborators, then the kinship chart should be left out of the publication. Ethical practice has meant, at times, that anthropologists have not written the dissertations or books that would have brought personal advancement but harm to those with whom they worked. Sometimes anthropologists find themselves with unanticipated ethical dilemmas. What if a person being interviewed mentions having engaged in an illegal activity? Are fieldnotes private or public? What if an ethnographer's work is used by a political faction to justify violent acts? Can an anthropologist really say that he or she can foresee no harmful effects of publishing (or not publishing) research results?

Not too many years ago, as I was driving down a highway, I saw a billboard in front of a church that was advertising the title of the sermon for the following Sunday. It read, "The Evil in Cultural Relativism." Although I was happy to see a term I use so frequently in introductory anthropology classes show up in another context in U.S. culture, I was distressed to see that it meant something bad to that Christian minister when it means something so good and important to anthropologists. This does not mean that religion and anthropology do not mix; that is another discussion, and a very rich one when it comes to cross-cultural perspectives on the sacred or intracultural debates on the origins of humanity, for example. The reason I bring it up here is to explain that in anthropology, cultural relativism does not mean "anything goes," which is a popular connotation. It means that we (going back to Franz Boas, at the beginning of the twentieth century) endeavor to understand a culture by its own logic or rules rather than our own (if they are different). This does not mean that we personally agree with every practice we study as anthropologists. **Ethical relativism,** in which a person suspends judgment on cultural practices and believes they are all equally valid, is separate from **cultural relativism,** in which a culture is not judged as good or bad but is understood using its own framework.[2] For example, an anthropologist may be observing cultural relativism to understand the practice of infanticide as it is explained by a practitioner and at the same time have a personal belief that infanticide violates **human rights.** Anthropologists come from many different cultural and religious backgrounds, and we have very different views on such questions as when human life begins and ends or whether female circumcision is a cultural right or a violation of a human right. There are ongoing debates about such issues at professional anthropology meetings, and anthropologists participate in United Nations conversations on international human rights. You might find it interesting to read the United Nations Universal Declaration of Human Rights,[3] which was signed in 1948 by representatives of 48 countries, including the United States. People in many current social movements are asking their own countries to observe this document, and it outlines the larger contract of respect within which we think and act as anthropologists.

In the past, some anthropologists have made what they thought at the time were ethical decisions that have been seen as unethical by others at the time or later, or that the anthropologists themselves came to view later as unethical. Because ethical decisions are context-dependent, views on how one should behave ethically can change. For example, Margaret Mead and several other U.S. anthropologists of her generation provided information about Pacific cultures in their work for the U.S. Office of Strategic Services (or military intelligence) during World War II, believing it to be the right way to use their professional knowledge for their country.[4] A few anthropologists worked for the Central Intelligence Agency during the Vietnam War. Such roles brought outcries from other anthropologists, who did not want the discipline to be associated with spying because our role as cultural observers can be uncomfortably confused with that "spy" role anyway. It also brings up a basic ethical issue related to **conflicts in accountability.** Were anthropologists who were working for the government during war working to promote anthropological understanding or to promote their government's ability to undermine another government? In a very different example of conflicting accountability, if an anthropologist is hired by a government to assess a social services program, is he or she working for the government or for the program (or for the discipline of anthropology, to throw in a third element)?

You can learn more about the history of anthropology and how we have, we hope, learned from our experiences in the discipline by reading the collections edited by Carolyn Fluehr-Lobban (1991) and Walter Goldschmidt (1979). Fluehr-Lobban discusses how anthropologists have drafted and redrafted ethical codes to reflect contemporary views, and she provides examples of them over time. A recent ethical controversy in anthropology that you might look into is the accusation by a journalist that several anthropologists acted unethically in their research among the Yanomami people in the Amazon region. Although the ethical codes of the discipline of anthropology were reassessed in view of this controversy, our professional organizations do not grant and remove licenses, as is the case with doctors and lawyers, so the charges have been taken up by the Venezuelan courts. If it is decided legally that the anthropologists were guilty of violating the human rights of Yanomami collaborators, then the views of those anthropologists who made this charge within the profession some years ago will have been validated. **Whistleblowing,** or speaking up about ethical and legal violations even when it puts one at risk of losing one's job or worse, involves ethical decision-making and a need for legislative and professional protection. This controversy has brought up questions about whose voices are heard by professional anthropologists because Yanomami elders were bringing some of the same charges before the journalist published his book, but fewer people seemed to be listening.[5] On the other hand, of course, the power of labeling someone as unethical brings up its own ethical (and legal) problems. What are the ethical responsibilities of anthropologists regarding passing along information (a charge of ethical misconduct, for example) about which they have no direct knowledge? One of our responsibilities is to be familiar with professional guidelines and to know how to find sources and procedures for ethical decision-making and conflict resolution rather than ignoring issues raised. In the future, indigenous nations and other polities probably will be making the guidelines for anthropological research permission much more distinct, whether anthropologists are "insiders" or "outsiders."

I have discussed your **responsibilities** as a student of anthropology to think ethically; what about your **rights?** The Code of Ethics approved in 1998 by the American Anthropological Association includes a section on the ethical responsibilities of anthropologists to students, including not discriminating "on the basis of sex, marital status, 'race,' social class, political convictions, disability, religion, ethnic background, national origin, sexual orientation, age, or other criteria irrelevant to academic performance." Sexual harassment and other abuses of power are forbidden by U.S. anthropologists' professional code and by legal codes that pertain to your institution of learning. Additionally, anthropologists who teach and belong to the American Anthropological Association are bound by its Code of Ethics to be available to students, counsel students about career opportunities, assist them in finding professional positions, and give fair credit and compensation for participation in their research.

Giving **credit** and **compensation** to anyone involved in anthropological research is an important ethical principle. This is an area of much discussion in the discipline. Should all anthropological work be coauthored by anthropologists and their collaborators? How is a shaman's knowledge of plant uses, for example, protected legally and in ethical codes as intellectual property, and how should an ethnobotanist compensate the individual or group for reproducing that knowledge? What if the information could be used by pharmaceutical companies to make a profit if an anthropologist published it? Indigenous activists have been working to secure intellectual property rights, and there are Web sites that anthropologists with ethical dilemmas can consult.[6]

Most professional anthropologists are working in occupations other than teaching, and so our ethical codes extend beyond the classroom. The first professional code for anthropologists in the United States was the Code of Ethics composed by a committee of the Society of Applied Anthropology in 1949. Margaret Mead chaired that committee, and the code was intended

> to advance those forms of human relationships which contribute to the integrity of the individual human being; to maintain scientific and professional integrity and responsibility without fear or favor to the limit of the foreseeable effects of their actions; to respect both human personality and cultural values; to publish and share new discoveries and methods with colleagues; those are the principles which should be accepted and which should be known to be accepted by all those who work in the disciplines affecting human relationships.[7]

More than 50 years later, anthropologists find that there are many more specific guidelines, usually legal codes, governing work both inside and outside of academia. The Native American Graves Protection and Repatriation Act **(NAGPRA)** of 1990, for example, has had a profound effect on the practice of archaeology, biological anthropology, and museum anthropology. Skeletal remains identified as Native American were required by an act of Congress to be **repatriated** (returned) to Native American nations (and some groups such as the Lakota volunteered to repatriate remains of those unidentified by specific nation) for **reburial** according to their custom. Because having skeletal remains of ancestors, sometimes obtained through violence or theft, on display violated most cultural customs, NAGPRA specified not only full repatriation by a deadline (now past) but also new guidelines for what to do when potential Native American remains are encountered during an archaeological excavation. Think about the ethics of anyone's ancestors' remains being displayed without permission, and consider how you feel about that.

Native American nations have specified which individuals can oversee decision-making and reburial as such situations arise. The response of the anthropological community to NAGPRA was not a simple one; some considered the reburial of collections to be a loss of potentially helpful scholarship. In some cases, there were collaborations between skeletal biological anthropologists, archaeologists, and Native American nations to learn what they could about the health and lifeways of the ancestors whose remains were in research collections before they were repatriated. Educational programs were established to share those results with those whose ancestors were reburied.

There are several ethical questions you might think about in relation to NAGPRA. What groups in the United States have controlled research collections? How have decisions been made in regard to reburying the remains in cemeteries or sending them to research institutions? Have the bodies of people seen as "white" or not poor been the most likely to be reburied in cemeteries instead of being sent to museums or being left unmarked under a construction site? What does it mean to have legislation that pertains to one ethnicity or set of political entities but not to others? What are the implications of NAGPRA for future research in anthropology? Does it encourage or discourage collaboration in research?

Anthropologists have an ethical obligation to share what we learn from our research and to do so honestly. What does that mean? You probably learned about plagiarism through student codes at your school, but beyond plagiarism there are other ways of being dishonest in reporting what we learn. What if a linguistic anthropologist uses a single example as representative of a shift in language practices without reporting the sample size? What if a map is drawn using a scale that misrepresents results? How can census figures be used properly? There are many ethical questions that arise in the collection and representation of data, whether those data are ways of pronouncing a word or the shape of shell mounds found along a sea coast. For this reason, most of the information presented to you in class has gone through a process called **peer review** or **intersubjective agreement,** in which a number of scholars agree that an article or book may be published because it represents a clear and current understanding of an aspect of anthropological knowledge. This process is subject to ethical dilemmas and constant revision, which is why your instructor and your textbook may not always agree on certain issues. It may also be why you are not allowed to include Internet sources that have not been subject to peer review in the references you use for assignments unless you are doing an analysis of such a site for other reasons.

How do anthropologists decide what is reliable information? This has changed over the decades. One example is the **insider/outsider debate** and the discussion of **objectivity.** Early in the history of the discipline, as anthropologists drew on the empirical tradition of the natural sciences to help form the methods of a new field of knowledge, "objectivity" was taken to mean the clarity of vision one can have through being an outside, or impartial, observer. Over time, anthropologists saw that our discipline is more complicated than that. We are not observing another species through a microscope; anthropologists are always humans learning about humanity from humans, and that puts us squarely into the picture, whether we admit it or not. Generations of feminist and postcolonial anthropologists introduced a new meaning of "objectivity" into the discipline: including multiple perspectives and making our own anthropological position explicit. The gender, native language, age, or nationality of the researcher may make a difference in what questions are asked and how they are answered. Whether to consider insider or outsider knowledge as more reliable continues to be a debate in the discipline, but most of us find we are a bit of both (insider and outsider) in any particular research context. Ethical questions here have to do with how we consider the research enterprise. Do we study others as objects of research? What does that imply regarding their rights as co-constructors of anthropological knowledge along with anthropologists (who may or may not be members of their own culture)? Does being an insider or outsider make a difference regarding the maintenance or disruption of stereotypes?

**Visual ethics** is a whole area of anthropological discussion currently under construction. Perhaps you will contribute to this discussion. It is possible to obtain informed consent when photographing an individual, but what should be done about permission in large group settings, such as a stadium or a political rally? Some have found ways to obtain informed consent in crowds, and some have argued that it is not possible to fully inform everyone about the photographer's intent. Can you think of a good way to do this? Professional guidelines in anthropology would lead us to the conclusion that a photograph or film footage taken without informed consent should not be reproduced by an anthropologist or shown to any audience. Some ethnographic films in the direct cinema tradition (that put the filmmaker into the frame) include discussions of this very issue. Are the photographs or film footage taken by anthropologists (including anthropology students) the intellectual property of the photographers or the property of the subjects of the images? Some anthropologists, on the consent form, give a date by which the people photographed may withdraw their consent. Anthropologists often provide an opportunity for the people filmed to view and comment on the film in a public venue and are ethically obligated to provide copies of images to those photographed. Given what was said earlier about the context-dependent nature of anthropological ethics, what do you think should be done about photographs and films made before informed consent became the practice? Should descendants be compensated for the use of their ancestors' images? Should these ethnographic materials no longer be available for public viewing?

There are many other ethical questions for students of anthropology to ask, and new ones are constantly arising as well. What does the Internet mean for the dissemination of images and research findings? How has the discipline both supported and challenged racism and eugenicist policy over the last century and a half? Is there a collaborative research process that can be relied upon to "keep us honest" in our research?

I hope that you can see, through the topics introduced in this chapter, that the discipline of anthropology has not made a steady progression from unethical to ethical practice, or the reverse, but as a community of researchers, teachers, students, and practitioners we constantly ask questions and often have disagreements about the most beneficial ways to proceed with our work as anthropologists. I encourage you to look at the Code of Ethics on the American Anthropological Association Web site to learn about relevant legislation, such as NAGPRA, and to ask yourself as you learn about the range of human experiences through anthropology course work how you are related to those you study and learn from through a contract of respect. Thinking anthropologically means thinking ethically as well.

## NOTES

1. I thank F. Michael McLain, my philosophical ethics professor two decades ago, for helping me locate the Sartre reference.
2. For a discussion of cultural, ethical, and epistemological relativism, see Whitaker (1996).
3. This Declaration of Human Rights may be found in May et al. (1988:30–33).
4. For further information, see Alcalay (1992).
5. For a description of one elder's visit to the American Anthropological Association meetings to speak with anthropologists about ethical practice, see Ritchie (1996).
6. See the International Society of Ethnobiology (ISE) Code of Ethics (http://users.ox.ac.uk/~wgtrr/isecode.htm).
7. This code is Appendix A in Fluehr-Lobban (1991).

## REFERENCES

ALCALAY, G.

1992. "The United States Anthropologist in Micronesia: Towards a Counter-hegemonic Study of *Sapiens.*" In *Confronting the Margaret Mead Legacy: Scholarship, Empire, and the South Pacific,* edited by L. Foerstel and A. Gilliam, pp. 173–203. Philadelphia: Temple University Press.

FLUEHR-LOBBAN, C., ed.

1991. *Ethics and the Profession of Anthropology: Dialogue for a New Era.* Philadelphia: University of Pennsylvania Press.

GOLDSCHMIDT, W., ed.

1979. *The Uses of Anthropology.* Washington, DC: American Anthropological Association.

MAY, L., S. COLLINS-CHOBANIAN, and K. WONG, eds.

1988. *Applied Ethics: A Multicultural Approach* (2nd edition). Upper Saddle River, NJ: Prentice Hall.

RITCHIE, M. A.

1996. *Spirit of the Rainforest: A Yanomamo Shaman's Story.* Chicago: Island Lake Press.

SARTRE, J.-P.

1948. *Existentialism and Humanism* (P. Mairet, trans.). London: Methuen.

WHITAKER, M. P.

1996. "Relativism." In *Encyclopedia of Social and Cultural Anthropology,* edited by A. Barnard and J. Spencer, pp. 478–82. New York: Routledge.

# Applying Anthropological Knowledge

*AARON PODOLEFSKY, University of Northern Iowa*

I would like to try an experiment, if you don't mind. Before you go on to the next paragraph, I'd like you to stop, look up from the page—close your eyes if you must—and ask yourself, "What are the three or four greatest problems facing America or the world today?" Take a few minutes to think about it. Jot them down on a piece of paper.

I have asked this question on the first day of my introductory anthropology classes for most of my career. Students take a few moments to think about the question, then, slowly, if I do not rush too quickly to fill in the silence, a few venture their personal opinions. As students share their short lists with each other, general discussion usually turns to considerations of the sorts of things that are repeated on the majority of the lists.

Students' concerns have changed somewhat over the years, but most themes seem to have remained reasonably constant. Students tend to see our biggest problems as crime, poverty, environmental issues, malnutrition and starvation (generally in the Third World), war, international and interpersonal conflict, discrimination based on "race" or gender, unemployment, AIDS, economic development, the global economy, or changing values (or unchanging values, depending on one's view). Today I expect terrorism or bioterrorism to be high on students' lists, as might be ethics in the corporate world. How does your list compare?

What is conspicuously absent are such things as how to make a faster computer chip, how to make cars more comfortable, how to make sure cell phones can reach us while we are backpacking, or so many of the other concerns that intrude into our daily lives.

What my students find terribly interesting is the degree to which the most frequently mentioned problems are social problems or have significant social dimensions. Class discussions usually lead to the students' realization that even problems that might at first seem not to be social in nature, such as environmental issues, have roots in social behavior. It soon becomes clear that the means for resolving or alleviating these problems probably also involves changes in social behavior or social policy. It always seems odd to me that this comes as such a surprise to so many.

Anthropologists often apply their knowledge and ways of thinking to questions like these (see Podolefsky and Brown 2002). Whether in the Third World or the First, addressing questions or concerns that have a direct impact on individuals' lives or affect society through changing social policies is what I call **applying anthropology.** Worded differently, applying anthropology involves using knowledge, methods, and anthropological ways of thinking to examine problems and issues of contemporary concern and to bring about change. This is a bit broader than the subfield of anthropology called applied anthropology, a subject usually included as the last chapter of introductory anthropology textbooks. From this broader point of view, you can apply anthropological thinking in business and in business classes (see Janus 1983; Labs 1992; Reeves-Ellington 1993) and in many other fields—even engineering, as in the development of crash dummies and ergonomic design (designing things so that people and things interact most efficiently and safely) (see Hertzberg 1979).

Distinguishing the application of a body of knowledge or methods from research into everyday questions is not unique to anthropology. Scientific work often is classified as basic research, applied research, and development. The distinctions are a bit fuzzy, but, as with most aspects of language, separating the concepts helps us think about the differences.

**Basic research** includes studies conducted to discover new knowledge for its own sake. That is, we want to know something because it is knowable, and humans should know whatever can be known. Investigation takes place without particular regard for a topic's practical importance or potential impact. In the end, of course, basic research creates knowledge that forms the foundation for understanding and enables researchers to think about more practical problems in new ways.

**Applied research** differs in that it examines problems and concerns that intentionally have a directly practical or instrumental outcome. Anthropologists who apply anthropology may work for clients who want to learn fairly specific things. For example, a medical examiner's office may engage a physical or biological anthropologist to assist them identifying long-buried bones that might be the remains of a missing person. Given their expertise, biological anthropologists may be able to make a good estimate about the height and properly assess the sex and "race," of the victim of a crime and, by applying their skills, help to identify the person (see Snow and Luke 1970). Anthropologists have worked on cases involving individual remains, airplane disasters, and mass grave sites (*Anthropology Newsletter* 1982; Huyghe 1988).

Applied research may also examine questions that are more sweeping. Some of my own work involved developing strategies for involving community groups in crime prevention activities (Podolefsky 1983; Podolefsky and DuBow 1981). Although my earlier work had focused on New Guinea highlands law, I was readily able to apply anthropological theories and methods to urban American settings, such as in Chicago. In applied work, anthropologists use the knowledge and methods developed over a hundred years of research in other cultures to develop policies and practices that can have significant implications for public policy.

**Development** is the use of knowledge derived from both basic and applied research to create (develop) approaches and means to solve problems. Different kinds of anthropologists have been involved in developing research-based programs or policies to ameliorate social problems. Archaeologists Alan Kolata and Oswaldo Rivera had spent a decade excavating in Bolivia when they recognized that the ancient, prehistoric societies in the region had used extensive irrigation canal systems to enhance crop growth. When the Spaniards came to South America, they brought their own "hacienda" system, which replaced the native "raised fields" system. The new system did not work very well in the high Andes on local potatoes. Kolata and Oswaldo enticed several local farmers to experiment with the old system, and the crop yield increased by 20 percent. Reintroducing this farming method was so successful that the Bolivian government is sponsoring the teaching of the technique to reduce the region's nutritional problems (Straughan 1991).

It is not how one thinks but what one thinks about that distinguishes applied anthropological thinking from other contexts of anthropological thinking. For students, applying anthropology means using the intellectual tools of anthropology to think about issues of contemporary concern at home and abroad. Applying anthropological thinking takes advantage of the fundamental knowledge generated through basic research, it uses the methods and theories of basic research, and it maintains the standards for explanation that apply to basic research. It follows that the nature of the thinking, in most respects, used to apply anthropology is very similar to the thinking strategies described in previous chapters.

One of the purposes of this chapter is to help you become more aware of your habits of mind. How do you approach and think about critical social questions? More fundamentally, do most of us even stop to ask about the linkages within a social system? We are not usually trained to think this way.

What if we asked questions about the simplest of things. For example, what was the effect of the introduction of air conditioning? That's easy. Everyone got cooler. True, but what else? When I was young (in the 1950s), before air conditioning was widespread, my grandparents spent hot New York City summer nights sitting with their neighbors on the steps outside their apartment building. Often they brought down card tables, and the men played cards and the women played Mahjong (a game played with tiles) until the apartments cooled off. Everyone knew everyone else, which led to social cohesion and mutual aid in difficult times. Today, the apartments are air conditioned, people do not congregate outside where it is cooler, and people in that same neighborhood hardly know their neighbors. Streets at night are occupied mostly by youths, and there is little supervision. Crime can occur with few to observe. Maybe air conditioning caused abandoned streets, which caused the increase in crime? Well, let's not go that far. But you can see that by looking at a common situation that occurred all over the country, one can speculate about a range of social consequences. So what happens to a small South American community when television is introduced? (See Pace 1993.) Or cell phones?

I believe that most people do not recognize social and cultural complexity. Because we all live within a society, it is intimately familiar. Everyday circumstances (or even rare events such as the introduction of air conditioning) do not call out for explanation. Rather, they simply are the way it is. This is not the case with all academic fields.

As an undergraduate, I earned a degree in mathematics. I was never involved in conversations with friends about mathematics. Odd as it may seem, I was intrigued by a number sequence called Fibonacci numbers. Outside a small group of classmates, no one was interested in talking about Fibonacci or the computer application to generate an approximation of pi. I never attended a party where someone struck up a conversation on any mathematically related topic. The reason was very clear: few people consider themselves sufficiently expert to discuss these complex problems (not to mention that it is boring to most folks). Everyone knows that special knowledge is needed to venture a rational opinion. Or so I believed.

I had just the opposite experience in the social sciences, particularly when I was researching urban crime. For example, I will bet that most of you had an opinion about whether air conditioning caused urban crime, but none ventured an opinion on Mr. Fibonacci.

People, society, and culture are familiar; we are enveloped in society in our everyday existence. This proximity leads people to believe they understand how society works, how it came to be the way it is, and how its institutions function. Everyone is an expert on culture, or so they think, but few see the complexity of social issues or even the potential for the link between factors that are not apparently related (air conditioning and crime). Commonly, people form opinions with no knowledge of social theory, evidentiary data, or comparison cases. This has long been a frustration to me, but it has grown worse in recent years. It seems more common these days to assert that one's opinion is one's own, and because it is "my opinion" it should not be subject to scrutiny by others because an opinion is an opinion and all opinions are equal. What is worse, people often don't really scrutinize their own opinions.

Don't get me wrong. Everyone has a right to his or her opinion. And I strongly advocate students having many passionate views. The function of education, of course, is to help you learn how to turn your and other opinions into suppositions (if not testable hypotheses) and to explore the validity of these suppositions.

It seems that because the questions, concerns, or problems of social sciences are commonplace, some assume that the answers or solutions must be simple or obvious. Ask anyone how to reduce crime in this country, and you will probably get a strongly held opinion. Some will immediately suggest longer jail terms, others will suggest reducing poverty, still others will advocate less violent television, and so it goes. One needs to ask, "Does increasing the length of jail sentences work as a deterrent to crime? How would I know? Are there data?"

Anthropology has some conspicuous advantages for helping students learn to think scientifically about social problems. It also has some disadvantages, but these can easily be overcome. Both the advantages and disadvantages result from the exotic nature of our subject. Unlike most other social sciences, anthropology's subject matter is unfamiliar; this is also true of biological anthropology that is more closely allied to the biological sciences. Unlike sociology and psychology, human evolution and archaeology are not part of our daily lives, and few students have spent much time in the far-off corners of the globe where most cultural anthropological field research is conducted.

The downside of this unfamiliarity is that the exotic (from our viewpoint) nature of life in Fiji, South Africa, or New Guinea can lead to a fascination with facts and descriptions to the exclusion of explanations. There is nothing wrong with a fascination about other lifeways (what people eat, how many husbands or wives they can marry at a time, how they wage warfare, or descriptions of their symbolic or religious lives). It is going beyond mere description that is critical.

The upside to this unfamiliarity—the anthropological advantage—is that students encounter a wide variety of social arrangements that beg to be explained. Once one has read and understood the description of a place, people, or social situation, the student's challenge is to remember to ask the question "Why." For example, one could read about the status of women in one or more societies and stop there. Or one could ask, "Why do women have equal status in some societies and not in others?" Or one could hypothesize that inequality is most common where women are economically dependent, and equality is most common where women are economically independent (Friedl 1978). Then one might ask, "If women's status is related to access to the economy, how might equality be fostered?"

In this example of women's status you can see that the last of these questions applies the knowledge of the first two to the solution of a practical problem. A possible solution to the last question might be to provide interest-free small business loans to women. This might work well in one setting, but what about doing this in India, for example? What might be the cultural impediments? What values, beliefs, and structures would have to be overcome for this to be successful? What are the roles of women in this society? Anthropologists have tackled these questions.

We apply anthropological thinking to questions that come to us because of our own interest or because others need to know answers. Policy makers may want to know how best to implement a local economic development program (Murray 1987) or how best to reduce the refuse in landfills (Harrison, Rathje, and Hughes 1975). Corporate executives may want to know how to understand another culture so that their managers can best work with managers from this culture (Reeves-Ellington 1993). There may be differences ranging from beliefs and values to how organizations are structured. Managers may want to know how to prepare their employees or their employees' spouses to live in another country (Trager 1987). Physicians or social service workers may need to know how to interact with new immigrants from other countries (Johnson 1991).

In each of these cases and many others that could be cited, it is important that someone first recognize these as issues or problems. The difficulties encountered by spouses of employees who are stationed overseas were long ignored, but ignoring the problem clearly led to low productivity. Why did this take so long to recognize?

Once issues such as these are recognized, people need to agree whether it is a problem that needs to be solved. There is an important but seldom recognized difference between **issues** and **problems.** An issue is something that equally well informed people will disagree about. A problem is a situation or condition that everyone agrees is unacceptable. We can apply anthropological thinking to both issues and problems, but we should recognize the difference and not be surprised that it is quite difficult to resolve issues.

Let's look for a moment at the question of women's access to family planning information and birth control in Third World countries (Schuler and Hashemi 1995). Is this an issue to be resolved or a problem to be solved? It is clear that even in cases in which a nation's population growth is staggering and malnutrition is common, agreement can be reached on the goal of reducing population growth. But decisions about how to reach this goal may be more difficult because it may be framed in terms of values. Once the decisions are made, the problem becomes how best to communicate family planning information. It turns out that this and similar efforts are much more difficult to achieve than it seems on its face.

It is important not only to think that good ideas about a program might solve a problem but also to address the frequently ignored question that we all need to worry about: did it work? Too often we have a good idea and then move on without asking the next question. In our family planning example, there are two goal levels. Once a program is designed, does it, in fact, disseminate the family planning information, and does it lead to lower rates of childbirth? How do we know? This is one of the major questions for evaluation research. It is enough here to point out that evaluating programs is a great way to test our understanding of society. Programs based on a sound analysis of the cause of a phenomenon, if well implemented, should be more successful than those that were based on poor theory.

Because cultural anthropologists have worked in so many different cultures, they have become sensitive to how **categories** are defined and how things are **counted.** It is a perspective that gives an important respect to an insider or native view of the world. What is a crime, for example? Or what constitutes divorce in a particular culture? Anthropologists, and other social scientists as well, sometimes run into difficulties because the words we use have common meanings that can create confusion. This happened to me as I was preparing for field research in the Papua New Guinea highlands. There was considerable disagreement about whether there was "law" in New Guinea. In 1958, Leopold Pospisil wrote that had he adopted a common anthropological definition, the systematic application of force, he would have reported that the Kapauku had no law. Klaus Koch (1970; 1974) studied warfare and concluded that military operations indicate the absence, inadequacy, or breakdown of other mechanisms, such as law, designed to reduce conflict. And Hatanaka (1973) reported that "the developed concept of 'law' and related notions are not easily applicable to activities in the traditional societies of New Guinea. There is a virtual absence of authority, leadership, and law as usually understood."

How, I wondered, could densely populated tribes of thousands of people live together without law? Were they "lawless"? I decided that worrying about the definition was limiting my thinking. I decided to investigate what people did when they had grievances or troubled cases. I found ample opportunity for research and discovered that highlanders have a variety of two-party and three-party strategies for conflict resolution that fit the needs of their culture and society (see Podolefsky 1992).

Anthropological thinking is a habit of mind that begins by questioning fundamental categories of meaning. It questions what things are lumped together and therefore asks fundamental questions about quantitative data. I was fascinated by a study that showed that what had been thought to be a steady rise in child abuse over a number of years turned out to be the result of changing definitions of child abuse, which resulted in an increase in instances that were counted. Similarly, in my study of urban crime prevention, I pointed out that programs that urge citizens to report crimes can cause the crime rate to go up because the crime rate is based on the count of reported crimes, not the actual number of crimes (which is unknown because many are not reported). Thus, a successful block watch program may cause the official crime rate to go up. Such modest complexities suggest that thinking anthropologically, especially where conclusions can have critical public consequences, requires us to look beyond the obvious into the social construction of data and social categories.

## CONCLUSION

No matter where we look around us, from Africa to the Middle East to our own nation, state, town, and neighborhood, there are complex and critically important issues that deserve our attention. Some are global policy issues that may affect the lives of millions of people. Others are local questions, such as whether a social program actually achieved its goal. This is important to know even if the program affects only a small number of people. What these have in common is that thinking about either requires habits of mind that allow people to see below the surface to the underlying themes of human behavior.

To apply anthropological knowledge, one must recognize patterns that lead to the application of theory and the generation of hypotheses. One must know how to collect data of various kinds and how to roll those data up into an understanding that goes beyond the mere summary of numeric or descriptive information.

What may be most important for you to know is that this intellectual ability does not come instantaneously. Academic skills and abilities come no easier than athletic skills. We know that a great swimmer or diver must practice hours each day. And so it is with the ability to apply anthropological thinking. Seek out opportunities. When you read a newspaper article about a nation in which women are not allowed to drive, go beyond merely saying, "Oh, that's their custom" or "Gee, that's not fair." Ask yourself, for example, how this affects their role in the family and in society. Ask yourself about the function of this custom for maintaining the social order (equality or inequality). Ask yourself how this social custom reinforces other social institutions such as religious and political practices. Ask yourself who benefits and who loses. And if you want to apply your thinking to creating change, ask yourself who will object if those women drive (the list may be longer than you think with challenges to long-held customs) and how the change you seek will affect other aspects of society and culture.

Applying anthropological thinking to complex issues takes incisive, penetrating, and rigorous thinking. Apply this standard to your thinking about other peoples and cultures. Then look in the mirror and apply it to your own.

## REFERENCES

AMERICAN ANTHROPOLOGICAL ASSOCIATION
  1982. "American Anthropological Association 1982 profile." *Anthropology Newsletter* 23–26.

FRIEDL, E.
  1978. "Society and Sex Roles." *Human Nature* 31–35, April.

HARRISON, G. G., W. L. RATHJE, and W. W. HUGHES
  1975. "Food Waste Behavior in an Urban Population." *Journal of Nutrition Education* 7(1):13–16.

HATANAKA, S.
  1973. "Conflict of Law in a New Guinea Highland Society." *Man* 8:59–73.

HERTZBERG, H. T. E.
  1979. "Engineering Anthropology: Past, Present, and Potential." In *The Uses of Anthropology*, edited by W. Goldschmidt. Washington, DC: American Anthropological Association.

HUYGHE, P.
  1988. "No Bone Unturned." *Discover* 9(12):38–45, December.

JANUS, N.
   1983. "Advertising and Global Culture." *Cultural Survival* 7(2):28–31.
JOHNSON, T. M.
   1991. "Anthropology and the World of Physicians." *Anthropology Newsletter,* Reprinted in Podolefsky and Brown (2002):271–74, November/December.
KOCH, K.
   1970. "Warfare and Anthrophagy in Jale Society." *Ibijdragen tot de taal-, Land- en Volkenkunde* 126:37–58.
   1974. *War and Peace in Jalimo.* Cambridge, MA: Harvard University Press.
LABS, J.
   1992. "Corporate Anthropologists." *Personnel Journal* 71(1):81–87, January.
MURRAY, G. F.
   1987. "The Domestication of Wood in Haiti: A Case Study in Applied Evolution." In *Anthropological Praxis,* edited by R. M. Wulff and S. J. Fiske. Boulder, CO: Westview Press.
PACE, R.
   1993. "First-Time Televiewing in Amazonia." *Ethnology* 32(2):187–205.
PODOLEFSKY, A.
   1983. *Case Studies in Community Crime Prevention.* Springfield, IL: Charles C. Thomas.
   1992. *Simbu Law.* New York: Harcourt Brace Jovanovich.
PODOLEFSKY, A. and P. J. BROWN
   2002. *Applying Anthropology: An Introductory Reader* (7th edition). New York: McGraw-Hill.
PODOLEFSKY, A. and F. DUBOW
   1981. *Strategies for Community Crime Prevention: Collective Responses to Crime in Urban America.* Springfield, IL: Charles C. Thomas.
POSPISIL, L.
   1958. *Kapauku Papuans and Their Law.* New Haven, CT: Yale University Press.
REEVES-ELLINGTON, R. H.
   1993. "Using Cultural Skills for Cooperative Advantage in Japan." *Human Organization* 52(2):203–15.
SCHULER, S. R. and S. M. HASHEMI
   1995. "Family Planning Outreach and Credit Programs in Rural Bangladesh." *Human Organization* 54(4):455–61.
SNOW, C. and J. L. LUKE
   1970. "The Oklahoma City Child Disappearances of 1967: Forensic Anthropology in the Identification of Skeletal Remains." *Journal of Forensic Sciences* 15(2):125–53.
STRAUGHAN, B.
   1991. "The Secrets of Ancient Tiwanaku Are Benefitting Today's Bolivia." *Smithsonian* 21(11):38–47.
TRAGER, L.
   1987. "Living Abroad: Cross-Cultural Training for Families." *Practicing Anthropology* 9(3):5–11.

# How to Take
# Anthropology Tests

MARY PULFORD, *Lake Superior College*
PATRICIA C. RICE, *West Virginia University*

Instructors and students agree on one thing: they hate to give and take exams. But, unfortunately, it is often the only way instructors can evaluate students, and because evaluation is a required part of your college career, it is never too early to think about testing. You probably received a syllabus for this class on the first day, so you already know which type of evaluation will be required during the term. In seminars and some upper-division courses, a lengthy term paper, usually based on library or original research, may be the only evaluation. But in introductory-level courses, you will be expected to take tests that will include one or some combination of multiple choice questions, true/false questions, short term identifications, and essays, short or long. This chapter will help you think about tests before, during, and after; it should help you with every test in this course and perhaps in other courses as well.

Test taking is a skill that can be enhanced by learning how to take them. Some students are "test smart," which means they find taking tests to be easy and even fun, and they do well on them. Other students do not do well on tests just because they are not "test smart." Two of you in this class may know the exact same things because you went to class every day, read the text, and even studied together, but one of you may do very well because you are "test smart" and the other may not do as well because until now, you were not as "test smart." Because being or not being "test smart" is not part of what instructors want to grade you on, we hope that this chapter will help to level the playing field. Remember that Einstein did not do well in school in Switzerland, perhaps because no one told him how to take tests.

But before we start making suggestions about how to take anthropology tests, you must be aware that test taking is close to the end of a progressive line; only the final grade and getting credit for the course comes after testing. We think it is important to start at the beginning of the process, to put taking tests in proper context. The first question to ask and answer is, "What is a test, and what does it purport to do?" Tests are questions that pertain to what you are expected to learn in a particular course, and taking a test entails answering those questions. We are not talking of comprehensive GRE (for entrance into graduate school), LSAT (for law school), or MedCAT (for medical school) tests, or the comprehensive tests some colleges give at the end of the senior year that attempt to evaluate a student's knowledge of an entire 4-year program. We are talking about tests for a particular course, such as the anthropology course you are enrolled in. Whether the test is short (a quiz) or long (a full hour or two), whether there will be three or four tests during the term or just a midterm and final, whether each exam or the final is comprehensive or not, the test will test your mastery of certain assigned materials. Normally that involves written materials (certain chapters in a textbook or assigned readings) and in-class materials (lectures, discussions, questions and answers, exercises); it may also involve assignments done on the Internet.

### Our Advice

Know what you will be tested on; check the syllabus and, if in doubt, ask your instructor. Read all of the written materials at least once when assigned, underlining or highlighting principles or what your instructor says to look for in the readings; reread either the entire assignment or your underlinings or highlightings before the test. Spend just as much time, if not more, on reviewing in-class materials. Do not miss class unless absolutely necessary. When making out a test, your instructor must assume you have been to every session. Remember that your instructor is a professional anthropologist, knows just as much as a textbook (if not exactly the same things in that textbook), and has put countless hours into finding good class materials, synthesizing many different perspectives and research articles, and is prepared for class. Your instructor therefore believes that what he or she presents in class is important. Most tests will cover both readings and in-class materials but may vary in how each will be weighed. Unless your instructor tells you to the contrary, assume that tests will weigh half on readings and half on class materials. If in doubt, ask your instructor.

Don't miss class, and take good notes. You need not write down every word your instructor says, but be sure you note all concepts, principles, and identifications, with enough detail to define them, because that is often what shows up on tests. Instructors often put key words and phrases on the chalkboard, so be sure to note them and their importance. If the instructor thinks they are important enough to put on the chalkboard, then they may show up on tests. If you must miss a class, get notes from someone who was there because it is better than a blank spot in your notebook. If you go to class every session and study your notes, you can get every in-class question correct on the test; if you get notes from someone else who was there, you probably will get half of the in-class questions right; if don't go to class and therefore can't study these materials, you may get 25 percent correct. Most multiple choice tests have four possible answers, so if you have nothing to study and are guessing at answers, you will average 25 percent correct. Because most essay questions are generated from in-class materials, you will probably do very poorly on essays that were based on topics discussed in class that you missed. There is a huge spread between 25 percent and 100 percent. You can't study in-class materials if you have nothing to study. It may feel good to not have anything to study at the time, but you will not be happy when you see the exam and your grade on it.

## MULTIPLE CHOICE QUESTIONS

Some exams are made up of only multiple choice questions; this is particularly true in large classes. Other tests are a mixed bag of some multiple choice questions and some essays, short or long. Multiple choice questions can vary from a lead statement with one correct clause to correctly complete the statement to questions that ask you to find two correct answers or decide whether all or none of the answers is correct. Some questions are negative questions with "not" or "never" in them; here you will have to decide which answers make correct statements and which one does not, which of course is the correct answer to that negative question. Some questions are factual, and some attempt to make you think about the answer. How do you take multiple choice tests?

If you don't go to class on a steady basis, you will have to guess at the answers, and if there are four possible answers, you can expect to get only 25 percent correct on that test. The rest of this discussion is based on the assumption that you are attending class regularly; otherwise, we cannot help you.

What follows is based on the assumption that your instructor wants to find out what you know and is not trying to trick you for some reason. Although there may be a few cases of attempted trickery out there, probably 99 percent of instructors want to find out what you know in order to assign appropriate, earned grades that are based on performance. Try to deconstruct the making of a test by putting yourself in the shoes of an instructor. Because instructors want to know how much you have mastered of those materials, when they sit down at their desks and contemplate making out tests, their thinking goes something like this: "How do I find out what the students know about topic X?" The answer to this question becomes a lead statement about topic X. For example, your instructor may decide he or she wants to find out whether you know about the relative distribution of Neandertal fossils and artifacts back 50,000 years ago. So, a question might be:

The largest number of Neandertal fossils has been found in
  (a) Italy        (c) Germany
  (b) Israel       (d) France

A negatively put question could be:

In all but which of the following places do we find Neandertal bones?
  (a) France       (c) Kenya
  (b) Israel       (d) Iran

Other questions can attempt to make you think through a question rather than regurgitate a memorized answer. Such a "thought question" might be:

Given the dates of fossils and artifacts of Neandertal and anatomically modern humans, the likely relationship between the two populations is
  (a) Neandertal and modern humans never met because the dates do not overlap.
  (b) Because the dates overlap a few hundred years but only in eastern Europe, they probably did not run into each other.
  (c) The dates overlap by thousands of years, and because only modern humans survived, it is likely that they killed off or outcompeted Neandertal.
  (d) The dates overlap by thousands of years, and they either ignored each other or made love, not war, as there is no evidence of conflict.

Instructors don't usually construct questions in full form. Rather, after they decide what they want to find out about what you know, they write the lead statement and then ponder the possible answers (clauses that complete the statement). One clause is easy: the correct one. The harder ones are the incorrect ones because they must be plausible to the student who has not done his or her work and is only guessing but obviously incorrect to the student who knows the correct answer. And that's how instructors make out multiple choice questions. Knowing how they do it may help you in taking their tests.

Let's assume you are a good student who has gone to class regularly, read the assigned readings, and studied for the test. Some students have no problem looking at each question with its possible answers and picking the correct one. They simply know it to be the correct answer and know that the others are incorrect. But remember that your instructor must construct answers that are not dead giveaways, and those "other three answers" may have bits of correctness in them. How do you handle that? Easy: don't look at the answers! Sometimes answers confuse students, although the lead statement doesn't. So if your test has the answers on a separate line from the lead statement, don't look at the answers, but mentally answer the question before looking at the choices given. Then it is usually easy to find the same answer you told yourself was correct from the answers provided. Or cover up the answers with your hand or a blank card if your eye wants to wander down to the answers, and do the same thing: tell yourself how to complete the lead statement, and then find it in the answer choices. Most multiple choice questions lend themselves to this treatment.

If you get in the habit of covering up the answers until you have mentally answered each lead statement question, you will find that you don't leave out questions, nor do you answer them too hurriedly. All too often students go over an exam after it has been turned back, come to a particular question, and say, "Oh, I read that too fast." Or, "I recognized a phrase in that particular answer, so I chose it." Don't look for recognizeable words; look at the complete statement. Usually without knowing it, instructors put recognizable words in incorrect choices, and they turn out to be *faux ami* (false friends).

Finally, most multiple choice questions are answered on mechanically graded answer sheets such as Scantron sheets. Far too many students leave one or two answers blank, mark two answers, or forget to do the last page of questions.

## Our Advice

Take a few minutes to go over your answers to see that you did not make any of these mistakes. Carefully erase your answers if you change your mind, and erase any notations you may have made on the sheet. The sheets are very sensitive to pencil (or they could not be graded) and pick up graphite very easily, and extraneous pencil marks may make your answers appear incorrect. Mechanically graded answer sheets are meant to save the instructor's time, so you cannot expect him or her to go over each test individually to make sure every question is answered or that there are no extraneous marks on the sheet. That's your job. Don't lose points this way.

## TRUE/FALSE QUESTIONS

True/false questions usually hinge on one or two words. Look for words such as "always," "never," and "seldom" because often the statement you have to judge as correct or incorrect hinges on whether the adverbial phrase is correct. (Multiple choice questions often use the same adverbs.) A statement such as "All humans have 23 chromosomes" is incorrect for two reasons: some humans have an extra chromosome, and humans have 23 **pairs** of chromosomes. If the statement said, "Most humans have 23 pairs of chromosomes," it would be correct. Remember that "all" means 100 percent, "most" means more than half, "some" means less than half, "a few" means less than 10 percent, and "none" means 0.

True/false questions often put two possibly linked items together and ask you whether they are linked. Sometimes, the linkage is between a place and a happening, as in "The Trojan Wars took place in Greece." If the linkage between the happening and the place is incorrect, then obviously the statement is false. If three things are linked, as in "The Trojan War took place in Greece in the third century AD," and either the time or place is incorrect, the statement is false. Sometimes the linkage is between the past and the present, as in "The Anasazi made kivas, but their modern descendants, the Hopi, do not." Sometimes the linkage is between two or more parts of some phenomenon, such as "Pottery and farming are always associated with sedentary life." But note that in each of these linkages, there is also a real or implied adverb such as "always" or "never." They are the words to look for.

## DEFINITIONS AND SHORT IDENTIFICATIONS

Often anthropological concepts and terms are so important that they must be internalized or memorized, and your instructor may ask you to identify some of them to make sure you have mastered them. You should highlight or underline all such important words in your in-class notes (and know the definitions) and use the glossary that normally is at the end of chapters in texts. That's usually where your instructor will get the words to ask you about in the first place. When you write them out, be clear and brief, but convey the gist of the term or concept. If you can say it slightly differently from your instructor or the text yet keep its precise meaning, this tells your instructor that you really understand the term.

## ESSAY QUESTIONS

You may find yourself in an anthropology class in which the instructor prefers essay questions as a method of assessing your knowledge or combines multiple choice with essay. Essay tests often are designed to test a student's overall knowledge, depth of comprehension of an issue or concept, and critical thinking skills. Many students panic at the thought of doing essay questions. Even if you haven't taken freshman composition yet or your writing skills are not quite what they should be, you can still do well on essay tests.

### Our Advice

Preparing for essay tests takes the same path as preparing for multiple choice tests: go to class, read all of the assignments, and take good notes. If the syllabus clearly states that essays test will be the standard, you would be advised to ask the instructor for a sample question or two. If you ask this question during class (at the appropriate time), the rest of your classmates will be thankful because they too are probably trying to figure out what kind of essay questions the instructor will ask. You might also consider asking the instructor two follow-up questions: what criteria will the instructor use to assess your essay? And what is the format for taking the essays? For example, will the instructor hand out sheets of paper with the questions and then a space to write, or will you be using a blue composition book? If you are required to answer the questions in a blue book, then you will probably be writing significantly longer and more complex essays. You might even ask the instructor whether she or he will pass out a number of real test questions beforehand

and then pick on test day what questions will be used. (The instructor might chuckle at this idea, but it is worth the effort to ask.)

You have gone to class, read all of the assignments, taken good notes, gotten some sample questions, and know the format for the essay test. Now what? Essay tests are designed to test your ability to explain in detail and in depth a particular issue or question. In cultural anthropology you might get an essay question like this: "Define the concept of enculturation and explain how this concept applies to the general notion of culture." You should start by defining in some detail the concept of enculturation, explain how it works, and discuss its impact on the individual; then give some examples from your own life and from readings or films. Then describe how enculturation affects the lives of individual adults and a group or society. You might end by comparing the enculturation of children in your own culture with that of another. Is the process the same, or are the outcomes different?

Here's another example: your instructor has spent some time talking about kinship and has used the Trobrianders as an example. (If your instructor uses a specific example in class, double check your readings because you might find follow-up information available.) A possible essay question might be, "Explain how kinship works among the Trobrianders." Begin by describing in general terms what kinship means, perhaps giving an example from your own culture. Then go into some detail about how kinship works among the Trobrianders. What are the implications for the Trobrianders of a particular type of kinship system? Does it affect their political or gender roles? How does kinship interrelate with the economic life of the Trobrianders? Your instructor does not want you to know just the standard definition of kinship; you should also know how this concept works in the daily life of a Trobriander. In other words, you need to demonstrate that you understand the concept and can apply it in general as well as to a specific culture.

Now you know how to think about answering an essay question in the area of cultural anthropology, but what about archaeology or physical anthropology? Aren't those two areas of anthropology only about facts? Hardly; read on.

Let's suppose you get the following question: "Define and discuss the implications of bipedal locomotion." To start, you need to define what it means to be a bipedal hominid. Remember that birds are bipedal, too! (They also walk upright on two feet.) You need to discuss how bipedalism works in hominid survival. What are the benefits to being bipedal? How do these benefits help both an individual and a group survive? Does being bipedal contribute to social organization in any way? What are the disadvantages of being a bipedal hominid? Think about it: bipedalism exerts great stress on the knees, legs, hips, lower back and feet. Do the advantages outweigh the disadvantages? If so, how and why?

### Our Advice

One of the best ways to take an essay test is not to write what you are thinking but to think about what you want to write. Just as in a speech class you prepare ahead of time for a speech and prepare a written outline. You should do the same for essay tests. Ask yourself, "What do I want to write? Do my sentences and paragraphs flow together to show that I really do understand the concept? Do my ideas flow together? How will I make my argument or build my case to answer the question?"

If your instructor provides sample questions or perhaps the real questions, take the time to think about an outline for answering those questions. You might even practice writing an essay answer. And then ask someone to read and critique it and reciprocate when that person needs the same kind of help.

One problem many students have who don't pre-think or outline their essay answers is that when they start to write, they write everything they know about an issue or question in one long paragraph. Fifty factual sentences strung together in one long paragraph isn't what your instructor wants to read. Can you connect those facts? Can you explain the big picture? What are the implications of all of those facts?

Ask your instructor before the test starts whether it is OK to make an outline of what you are going to write on the test sheet. This way, you will think about what you want to say and clear your mind of hundreds of unrelated facts. If your instructor says "No," just make a mental outline.

### Our Advice

Write clearly. Good handwriting or printing is a must here. If your instructor cannot read your handwriting, no matter how great the content is, your grade might suffer. Also, stay away from fluorescent ink. These colors may be difficult to read and, like poor handwriting, become a distraction. Use a good pencil or black or blue ink. Always have a good eraser that you know works! Take your time reading and answering the test; even if others are finishing before you, you don't have to rush. If you have an hour to do the test, use the entire hour if needed. Try to get to the classroom 10 to 15 minutes before the test starts. This way, you can get settled, clear your mind, and prepare yourself mentally.

Finally, read over your essays. You may think it is perfectly clear as you are writing, but a reread may find missing words, poor grammar, or a lapse of continuity. If you don't reread it, you can't correct it. It is worth the extra minute or two to reread your answers.

### AFTER THE EXAM

What if you didn't do well on your first test, regardless of whether it was multiple choice or essay? You should look carefully over your test to see where there is room for improvement. Did the instructor make notes on your essays that would be helpful for the next test? Did you misplace a mark on the Scantron sheets? Were you properly prepared? A visit to your instructor during his or her office hours might help you improve your next test score. And you might consider a group study session for the next test. Some students do better studying alone, and some do better studying with other students preparing for the same exam. If your study habits for the first exam paid off with a good grade, stick with them. If not, consider changing to another method.

Finally, don't let one bad grade turn you off in a course. Most instructors consider grade improvement in a positive light and are very willing to help you improve your scores. Sometimes a certain kind of testing does not indicate how much you know; if this is true for you, feel free to discuss this with your instructor because there may be another way to test what you do know. Don't wait until the day before the last exam and then tell your instructor that you're having trouble. Improvement starts with the second exam.